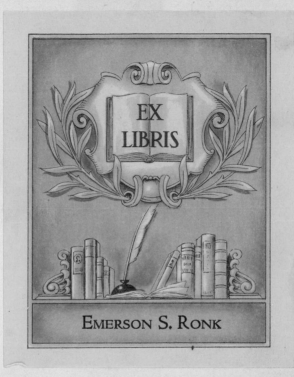

EX
LIBRIS

EMERSON S. RONK

Books by Gore Vidal

Novels

Williwaw (1946)

In a Yellow Wood (1947)

The City and the Pillar (1948)

The Season of Comfort (1949)

A Search for the King (1950)

Dark Green, Bright Red (1950)

The Judgment of Paris (1952)

Messiah (1954)

Short Stories

A Thirsty Evil (1956)

Plays

Visit to a Small Planet and Other Television Plays (1956)

Visit to a Small Planet (1957)

The Best Man (1960)

Essays

Rocking the Boat (1962)

Rocking
the
Boat

Rocking
the
Boat

ꝫ BY GORE VIDAL

Little, Brown and Company
Boston · Toronto

The author wishes to thank the following for permission to
include articles first published by them: *Esquire, The Nation,
New York Herald Tribune, New York Times, New World
Writing, Partisan Review, The Reporter, Theatre Arts, Time, Inc.*

*Published simultaneously in Canada
by Little, Brown & Company (Canada) Limited*

PRINTED IN THE UNITED STATES OF AMERICA

For

Joanne and Paul

FOREWORD

Thuese pieces dealing with politics and writing and
the theater were written during the last fifteen years.
I despair of giving them any significant order or of finding any great consistent line to what, after all, is the
work of many different occasions and moods. I have
included a certain amount of political journalism, knowing perfectly well that it ages before one's eyes, from
sentence to sentence. Yet I believe that if the political
comment has some relevancy to readers now and in
1962, then I am willing to risk boring the reader of 1963,
not to mention later.

Rereading one's own past commentary is like going
through an album of old photographs. Did I really part
my hair in that peculiar way? Was I ever that thin?
That self-conscious? I have kept several unflattering
snapshots in the interest of truth, and I have done almost no touching-up. I was struck, however, by the

fact that as I get older I find myself worrying more about "usefulness" and "relevancy" in writing. When I was younger literature in itself and for itself seemed to me to be quite enough. At moments in this book I sound like a dogged social realist and moralist pregnant with an extremely long and dispirited novel about the effect of the New York milk marketing order on the financial structure of a village in Scoharie County. For those who do not know my novels, I am not really that sort of writer. I invent rather than record. Nor do I demand that the novel, necessarily, have a social purpose. Perhaps what I am trying to say is that in a difficult age each of us, artist or not, must have some sense not only of social purpose but of moral priority. My adventures in practical politics (which I discuss in a number of pieces) convinced me of the need, simply and unpietistically, for right action. But each must write his own prescription; effective or not, I have written mine. Athens quarreled with Sparta over the small and unimportant city of Corcyra. The Peloponnesian War began and our world's first civilization was shattered.

In searching for a title for this collection I was tempted to use "Toward Corcyra," but I rejected it partly because it sounded too obviously portentous, partly out of latent hope. Yet many of these pages are shadowed by the thought of war and the extinction of man. Mr. William Faulkner may decline to accept our terminus, but I suggest that some sort of positive action is called for. Stylized despair is luxurious and dangerous.

I cannot read Thucydides today for, as his narrative

approaches the tragedy of Corcyra, one sees plain as death beyond that silver prose to some Corcyra of our own, and the world's end. It is useful to imagine the worst. But even as one anticipates the final nightmare of our race, something in the blood says: *No, not yet, life will prevail somehow.* To help life prevail is a reasonable thing to want to do, and it may be done by writing *Light in August,* or by attempting to change wrong laws, or by writing criticism.

I realize I am not easily placed, politically or critically. I once found myself staring with empty mind into a television camera as, presumably, millions of bored strangers stared back. I had been asked what my political philosophy was. Was I liberal or conservative? Or what? After a moment of panic, I heard myself say in that grave, somewhat ponderous voice television seminars summon from one's viscera: "I am a correctionist. If something is wrong in society, it must be fixed. At least one should try to fix it." In addition to this somewhat simpleminded social meliorism, I was early influenced or, perhaps, heartened by something George Santayana said to me. In 1948 he was living in the Convent of the Blue Nuns at Rome. I would visit him in his hospital room, and he would talk and I would listen — and try to remember everything he said, for at the end of the day I would write it all down in a notebook. We got on well; he was tolerant; he would answer my questions, but he never asked me a personal question and I'm not sure if he ever bothered to learn my name. But this was as it should be: he was eighty-five and I was twenty-three. He was the master; I was the pupil. When it came time for me to leave Rome, I said good-by to him. He walked with me down the corridor to the main door. He was small and fragile with glittering black eyes; he wore a dressing gown, a Byronic shirt open at the collar and a faded waistcoat of the 1890's. At the door to the hospital we shook hands. Then, as I was halfway through the door, he said, "I think you will have a happy life." I stopped and turned, not knowing what to say. He gave me a mischievous smile and added: "Because you lack superstition." We parted and I never saw him again. But I have often thought of what he said. I took it as a benediction laid on with the left hand, but secretly I have hoped it was a prophecy. So far it has proved true.

October 10, 1961
BARRYTOWN, N. Y.

CONTENTS

x i i i

C O N T E N T S

POLITICS

Political journalism is new to me. I find it a satisfying form of expression, even though it ages as fast as the newsprint that records it. In my *Esquire* columns I found, I think, an audience which was genuinely interested in public matters, and I kept largely to the field of civil liberties. In revising the pieces, I have tried to take out as much as possible those contemporary references which in a year or two make most political journalism mysterious to read. But I have kept everything else, including errors of prophecy.

JOHN KENNEDY: A TRANSLATION
FOR THE ENGLISH

UNTIL LAST MONTH (March, 1961), I had not been at the White House since 1957, when I was asked to compose a speech for President Eisenhower.

At that time the White House was as serene as a resort hotel out of season. The corridors were empty. In the various offices of the Executive (wings contiguous to the White House proper) quiet gray men in waistcoats talked to one another in low-pitched voices.

The only color, or choler, curiously enough, was provided by President Eisenhower himself. Apparently his temper was easily set off; he scowled when he stalked the corridors; the Smile was seldom in evidence. Fortunately, Eisenhower was not at the White House often enough to disturb that tranquillity which prevailed, no matter what storms at home, what tragedies abroad.

Last month I returned to the White House (a de-

3

feated Democratic politician, full of pluck) to find the twentieth century, for good or ill, installed. The corridors are filled with eager youthful men, while those not young are revitalized.

As Secretary of Commerce Luther Hodges (at sixty-two the oldest member of the Cabinet) remarked: "There I was a few months ago, thinking my life was over. I'd retired to a college town. Now . . . well, that fellow in there" (he indicated the President's office) "he calls me in the morning, calls me at noon, calls me at night: *Why don't we try this? Have you considered that?* Then to top it all he just now asks me: *Where do you get your suits from?* I tell you I'm a young man again."

In the White House press room reporters are permanently gathered. Photographers are on constant alert and television cameramen stand by, for news is made at all hours.

The affection of the press for Kennedy is a phenomenon, unique in Presidential politics. There is of course the old saw that he was a newspaperman himself (briefly, for INS) and also that he is a bona fide intellectual (on the other hand, the working press is apt to be anti-intellectual); but, finally, and perhaps more to the point, Kennedy is candid with the press in a highly personal way. He talks to journalists easily. There is no pomp; there is little evasion; he involves them directly in what he is doing. His wit is pleasingly sardonic.

Most important, until Kennedy it was impossible for

4

anyone under fifty (or for an intellectual of any age) to identify himself with the President. The intellectual establishment of the country opted for "alienation," the cant word of the 1940's and 1950's, and even those who approved of this or that President's deeds invariably regarded the men set over us by the electorate as barbarians (Truman's attack on modern painting, Roosevelt's breezy philistinism, Eisenhower's inability to express himself coherently on any subject).

For twenty years the culture and the mind of the United States ignored politics. Many never voted; few engaged in active politics. Now everything has changed. From Kenneth Galbraith to Robert Frost the intellectual establishment is listened to and even, on occasion, engaged to execute policy.

Close to, Kennedy looks older than his photographs. The outline is slender and youthful, but the face is heavily lined for his age. On the upper lip are those tiny vertical lines characteristic of a more advanced age. He is usually tanned from the sun, while his hair is what lady novelists call "chestnut," beginning to go gray. His eyes are very odd. They are, I think, a murky, opaque blue, "interested," as Gertrude Stein once said of Hemingway's eyes, "not interesting"; they give an impression of flatness, while long blond eyelashes screen expression at will. His long fingers tend to drum nervously on tables, on cups and glasses. He is immaculately dressed; although, disconcertingly, occasional white chest hairs curl over his collar.

5

The smile is charming even when it is simulated for the public. Franklin Roosevelt set an unhappy tradition of happy warriors, and ever since his day our politicians are obliged to beam and grin and simper no matter how grave the occasion. Recently, at a public dinner, I had a thoughtful conversation with Harry Truman. He was making a particularly solemn point when suddenly, though his tone did not change, his face jerked abruptly into a euphoric grin, all teeth showing. I thought he had gone mad, until I noticed photographers had appeared in the middle distance.

As for Kennedy's personality, he is very much what he seems. He is withdrawn, observant, icily objective in crisis, aware of the precise value of every card dealt him. Intellectually, he is dogged rather than brilliant.

Over the years I've occasionally passed books on to him, which I thought would interest him (including such arcana as Byzantine economy). Not only does he read them but he will comment on what he's read when I see him next (our meetings are casual, at long intervals, and I am happy to say that I have no influence).

After his defeat for the Vice-Presidential nomination in 1956, he was amused when I suggested that he might feel more cheerful if every day he were to recite to himself while shaving the names of the Vice-Presidents of the United States, a curiously dim gallery of minor politicians. Also, somewhat mischievously, I suggested that he read *Coriolanus* to see if he might find Shakespeare's somewhat dark view of democracy

6

consoling. Mrs. Kennedy and he read it aloud one foggy day at Hyannisport. Later he made the point with some charm that Shakespeare's knowledge of the democratic process was, to say the least, limited.

On another occasion, I gave him the manuscript of a play of mine whose setting was a nominating convention for the Presidency. He read the play with interest; his comments were shrewd. I recall one in particular, because I used it.

"Whenever," he said, "a politician means to give you the knife at a convention, the last thing he'll say to you, as he leaves the room, is: 'Now look, Jack, if there's *anything* I can do for you, you just let me know!' That's the euphemism for 'You're dead.' "

Kennedy's relationships tend to be compartmentalized. There are cronies who have nothing to do with politics whom he sees for relaxation. There are advisers whom he sees politically but not socially. The only occasion where personal friendship and public policy appear to have overlapped was in his appointment of the perhaps not distinguished Earl Smith (our envoy to Cuba at the time of the Batista debacle) as Ambassador to Switzerland. The Swiss, who were acting for the United States in Havana, complained loudly. To save the President embarrassment, Smith withdrew. With chilling correctness, Kennedy is reported to have called in the Swiss Ambassador to Washington and given him a lesson in international diplomacy (i.e. you do not criticize publicly an ambassadorial appointment without

7

first apprising the Chief of State privately). The Ambassador left the White House shaken and bemused. Immediately afterwards, an aide entered the President's office to find him beaming. "That was very satisfying," he said.

Kennedy is unique among recent Presidents in many ways. For one thing, he has ended (wistfully one hopes, forever) the idea that the Presidency is a form of brevet rank to be given a man whose career has been distinguished in some profession other than politics or, if to a politician, one whose good years are past, the White House being merely a place to provide some old pol with a golden Indian summer.

Yet the job today is literally killing, and despite his youth, Kennedy may very well not survive. A matter, one suspects, of no great concern to him. He is fatalistic about himself. His father recalls with a certain awe that when his son nearly died during the course of a spinal operation he maintained a complete serenity: if he was meant to die at that moment he would die and complaint was useless.

Like himself, the men Kennedy has chosen to advise him have not reached any great height until now. They must prove themselves *now*. Government service will be the high point of their lives, not an agreeable reward for success achieved elsewhere. Few men have the energy or capacity to conduct successfully two separate careers in a lifetime, an obvious fact ignored by most Presidents in their search, often prompted by vanity or a sense of public relations, for celebrated advisers.

Nearly half the electorate was eager to find Kennedy and his regime "intellectual" in the popular pejorative sense, given to fiscal irresponsibility and creeping socialism. (There is, by the way, despite the cries of demagogues, no operative Left in the United States. We are divided about evenly between conservatives and reactionaries.) But now, having experienced his Administration, it is evident even to the most suspicious of the Radical Right that Kennedy is not an adventurous reformer of the body politic, if only because this is not the time for such a reformation, and he knows it.

Essentially, he is a pragmatist with a profound sense of history, working within a generally liberal context. Since the United States is in no immediate danger of economic collapse, and since there is no revolutionary party of Left or Right waiting to seize power, our politics are firmly of the Center. The problems of the nation are a lagging economic growth, which under an attentive Administration can be corrected, and foreign affairs, where the United States *vis-à-vis* Russia remains a perhaps insoluble problem, but one to which Kennedy is addressing himself with coolness and a commendable lack of emotion.

Perhaps Kennedy's most unusual gift is an objectivity which extends to himself. He can discuss his own motives with a precision not usual in public men, who tend to regard themselves tenderly and according to the rhetoric of the day.

Before the primaries last spring, when his main opponent for the nomination was the attractively exuberant Senator Hubert Humphrey, Kennedy remarked privately that the contest was really one of temperaments, of "images," and though he confessed he did not have the Senator's passion for liberal reform, he did not think that was what the country in its present mood wanted or needed. Kennedy admitted to being less interesting and less dramatic than Humphrey, but for this time and place he felt he himself would prove more appealing, a correct if unflattering self-estimate.

Kennedy is certainly the most accessible and least ceremonious of recent Presidents. After last month's conference with the Canadian Prime Minister, the two men appeared in front of the White House for the usual television statement. Kennedy said his few words. Then he turned to the Prime Minister and said: "Now you make your statement while I go back to the office and get your coat." And the Prime Minister made his statement and the President got his coat for him.

A few days later, when Eleanor Roosevelt came to see him at the White House, he insisted that she allow him to show her her old home. As they were about to leave his office, he motioned for her to precede him through the door.

Mrs. Roosevelt drew back. "No," she said. "You go first. You are the President."

He laughed. "I keep forgetting." With her lovely, deliberate blandness, she replied, "But you must *never* forget."

Perhaps the most distressing aspect of the last Administration was President Eisenhower's open disdain of politics and his conviction that "politician" was a dirty word. This tragic view is shared even now by the majority of the American electorate, explaining the General's continuing appeal. Time and again during those years one used to hear: "O.K., so he is a lousy President, but thank God he's not a politician!"

Kennedy, on the other hand, regards politics as an honorable, perhaps inevitable, profession in a democracy. Not only is he a master of politics, but he also takes a real pleasure in power. He is restless; he wants to know everything; he wanders into other people's offices at odd hours; he puts in a ten-hour office day; he reads continuously, even, it is reported, in the bathtub.

Most interesting of all, and the greatest break with tradition, have been his visits to the houses of friends in Washington, many of them journalists. Ever since the first protocol drawn up for George Washington, the President seldom goes visiting and never returns calls. Kennedy has changed that. He goes where he pleases; he talks candidly; he tries to meet people who otherwise might never get to him through the elaborate maze of the White House, in which, even during the most enlightened Administration, unpleasant knowledge can be kept from the President.

Inevitably, a President is delivered into the hands of an inner circle which, should he not be a man of considerable alertness and passion, tends to cut him off from reality. Eisenhower was a classic case. It was painfully evident at press conferences that he often had no knowledge of important actions taken by the government in his name; worse still, he was perhaps the only President not to read newspapers. The result was that when crises occurred, despite good intentions, he was never sufficiently aware of the nature of any problem to have a useful opinion as to its solution.

Only by constant study and getting about can a President be effective. As Harry Truman once remarked, despite the great power of the office, it is remarkably difficult to get anything done. "You tell 'em what you want and what happens? Nothing! You have to tell 'em five times."

The reason for this seeming disobedience is due partly to the hugeness of the Federal government and partly to the fact that no matter what a President wants there are those who will oppose him within his own Administration. Most Presidential staffs inevitably take advantage of their President, realizing that in the rush of any day's business he will make many decisions and requests which he cannot possibly follow up. Kennedy, however, has already shown an unusual ability to recall exactly what he requested on any subject, and the impression he gives is of a man who means to be obeyed by his staff.

"He is deliberately drawing all the threads of executive power to himself," remarked one close adviser. The cumbersome staff system of the Eisenhower Administration has been abandoned in favor of highly personal relationships between President and advisers. No one's function is ever clearly defined. The President moves men from project to project, testing them, extracting new points of view.

Not only is this a useful way of getting the most out of his staff, but it also ensures, rather slyly, Kennedy's own unique position at the center of the web of power: he alone can view and manipulate the entire complex of domestic and international policy. No one in his Administration may circumvent him, because none can master more than a part of the whole.

This ultimate knowledge of the whole is power, and, finally, the exercise of power is an art like any other. There is no doubt of John Kennedy's mastery of that art. He is a rare combination of intelligence, energy and opportunism. Most important, he is capable of growth. He intends to be great.

What he will accomplish depends largely upon his ability to rally the bored and cynical Western world, to fire the imagination of a generation taught never to think of "we" but only of "I." There are fragile signs (the warm response to the Peace Corps) and favorable omens (popular approbation reflected in polls) that a torpid society has at last been stirred by its youthful leader. If true, it is in the nick of time. Civilizations are seldom granted a second chance.*

[*Sunday Telegraph* (London), April 9, 1961.]

* See Note 1 in the Appendix.

BARRY GOLDWATER: A CHAT

Julius caesar stood before a statue of Alexander the Great and wept, for Alexander at twenty-nine had conquered the world and at thirty-two was dead, while Caesar, a late starter of thirty-three, had not yet subverted even his own state. Pascal, contemplating this poignant scene, remarked rather sourly that he could forgive Alexander for wanting to own the earth because of his extreme youth, but Caesar was old enough to have known better.

I suggest, with diffidence, that Pascal did not entirely understand the nature of the politician; and the inner mechanism of a Caesar is no different in kind from that of an Alfred M. Landon. The aim of each is power. One would achieve it through military conquest, the other through what it pleases us to call the democratic process. It is natural for men to want power. But

15

to seek power actively takes a temperament baffling to both the simple and the wise. The simple cannot fathom how any man would dare presume to prevail, while the wise are amazed that any reasonable man would *want* the world, assuming he could get it.

Suspended then between simplicity and wisdom, self-delusion and hard practicality, is the operative politician. He is not at all like other men, though he must acquire as protective coloration the manners of his society, join in its rituals (Caesar, the atheist, was a solemn high priest and our own Calvin Coolidge wore an Indian war bonnet), exploit its prejudices and anticipate its hungers.

Like his predecessors, an American politician in the mid-twentieth century must conform to certain conventions. He must be gregarious (or seem to be), candid (but never give the game away), curious about people (otherwise, he would find his work unendurable). An American politician must not seem too brainy. He must put on no airs. He must smile often but at the same time appear serious. Most disagreeable of all, according to one ancient United States Senator, wise with victory, "is when you got to let some s.o.b. look you straight in the eye and think he's making a fool of you. Oh, that is gall and wormwood to the spirit!" Above all, a politician must not sound clever or wise or proud.

Finally, the politician must have that instinctive sense of occasion which is also the actor's art. To the right challenge he must have the right response. He is, in the purest sense, an opportunist. He must be an accurate barometer to the weather of his time. He must know the phases of the political moon and the hour of the tides. He must be ready at a moment's notice to seize that prize which is the game's reward, power. He must know in the marrow of his bones when it is right to make the large effort. For example, at the Democratic convention of 1956 the Vice-Presidential nomination was unexpectedly thrown open to the floor. The young Senator from Massachusetts went for the prize. The moment was wrong but the move was right. In a car on his way to the convention the day of the voting, John Kennedy was heard muttering grimly to himself, "Go, go, go!" When to go, when to stay; that is the art.

Even those who write knowledgeably about politics tend to make certain fundamental errors. They look for subtle motives where there are none. They believe there is a long-range plan of war when there is seldom anything more than quick last-minute deployments of troops before unscheduled battle. In a society like ours, politics is improvisation. To the artful dodger rather than the true believer goes the prize.

The junior Senator from Arizona, Barry Goldwater, is a politician of some grace and skill who at this moment is studying the political sky for omens, waiting for a sign in which to conquer. His moment may come in the Presidential election of 1964 or of 1968 or never. There is every evidence that he is, this year, a divided man, uncertain how to proceed. His sense of occasion is keen; his sense of history is practical. He knows perfectly well that his views are at variance with the majority views of his time. To do great deeds, to take the prize, he must, paradoxically, surrender many of those positions he has so firmly taken in his reaction to a society he neither likes nor, many feel, understands. Yet, again paradoxically, his entire celebrity is due to his appealingly cranky rejection of those positions the majority reveres. In short, he is loved for those very attitudes which a majority of the electorate does not accept.

Goldwater's success is phenomenal considering that he is only a second-term Senator with no significant legislation to his name. He comes from a politically unimportant state. By his own admission he is not a profound thinker. His success in Arizona was due not only to his charm and hard campaigning in a state usually Democratic but also to the popularity of his family, one of the oldest in the state, whose business, Goldwater's department stores, is to Arizona what Macy's is to New York.

It is a clue to Goldwater's recent success that he was primarily a salesman in the family business (his one creative contribution was the invention and promotion of men's shorts decorated with large red ants in the pants) and he considers his role at the moment as salesman for the conservative point of view, which is not necessarily the Republican view. But, spokesman for the majority of his party or not, bumper stickers with GOLDWATER IN '64 are beginning to appear around the country (as well as a few GOLDWATER IN 1864 stickers).

Goldwater's path to higher office is strewn with many hazards, not all of his own making. His father was Jewish (the family name originally was Goldwasser), yet he is an Episcopalian. Since he favors right-to-work laws and limitations on unions, organized labor is against him. Personally, he sees nothing wrong with Negro and white children together in the same schools. But he opposes permitting the Federal government to interfere with the rights of the Southern states to maintain segregation, even in the face of the Supreme Court's decision. Goldwater has about as much chance of getting the Negro vote, according to one Tennessee politician, as "a legless man in a pants-kicking contest." Reluctantly, Goldwater realizes that Social Security is here to stay — it is too late to take it away — but he does think the program should be voluntary and certainly not enlarged to include medical care for the aged or anything else. He favors breaking off diplomatic relations with the Russians; he wants to present them wherever possible with a take-it-or-leave-it, peace-or-war attitude which many thoughtful conservatives who approve his domestic program find disquietingly like brinkmanship. In his own party he is blocked not only by the attractive and liberal Nelson Rockefeller but by that moderate near-winner Richard Nixon.

As if all these difficulties, inherent and assumed, were not enough, he is now seriously endangered by his admirers. Like most radicals of Right or Left, he is attractive to every sort of extremist. His most compromising support comes from the mysterious John Birch Society, whose beleaguered "Founder" (a title last used by the creator of Hollywood's Forest Lawn Cemetery), Robert Welch, is firmly convinced, among other odd notions, that forty million Americans are Communists, including such unexpected conspirators as Milton and Dwight D. Eisenhower. Stubbornly, Goldwater has refused to repudiate the Birch Society, a stand which has led one Republican leader to say, "That's the end of Barry."

Yet, despite great handicaps, Goldwater is perhaps the country's most popular politician, after Kennedy. He gets enormous crowds wherever he goes. They are enthusiastic and — hopeful sign — they include many young people. He has caught on as a personality even if his policies have not. It is common to hear, "O.K., so a lot of his ideas are cockeyed, but at least he tells you where he stands. He isn't afraid to speak up, the way the others are." That many of Goldwater's ideas are in a state of flux and that many of his positions are quite as obscure as those of any other politician does not penetrate. Once a man's "image," good or ill, is set in the public's mind, he can contradict his legend every day and still be noted for his consistency.

Yet Goldwater *is* something new on the scene. He is perhaps the first American politician who, though spokesman for an unpopular minority, finds himself personally popular for reasons irrelevant to his politics. People like him as they like Arthur Godfrey or Jack Paar, forgiving the autocracy of the one and the tantrums of the other in precisely the same way they forgive Goldwater when he speaks against the $1.25 minimum wage, union activities or the Supreme Court's power to integrate schools. So what? He's a nice guy, and nice guys are not dangerous. He is also sincere, a vague quality far more admired by the lonely crowd than competence or intelligence.

Barry Goldwater's office is on the fourth floor of the old Senate Office Building. The corridors are marble with high ceilings and enormous doors which tend to dwarf not only visitors but Senators. There is an air of quiet megalomania which is beguiling in its nakedness.

Behind the great mahogany door with its sign Mr. Goldwater, Arizona is the outer office: wooden paneling, a view through large windows of the Capitol grounds. I was greeted by the Senator's secretary, Mrs. Coerver. She is small, amiable, gray, with that somewhat fixed smile politicians and their aides develop. (One smile is a vote gained, maybe. One frown is a vote lost, definitely.) "The Senator will see you in just a moment." She beamed.

I approached this meeting with curiosity. For one thing, since his book, *The Conscience of a Conservative*, Goldwater's fundamentalist ideas about the Constitution and society had undergone changes. When the Presidential virus attacks the system there is a tendency for the patient in his fever to move from the Right or the Left to the Center where the curative votes are, where John Kennedy now is. Other observers of Goldwater had also detected a perceptible shift to the Center. Further shifts would depend entirely on whether the patient took a turn for the White House. I wanted, simply, to take his temperature as of that day, for like all illnesses the Presidential virus has its own peculiar ebb and flow. At night in the company of good friends the fever blazes. In a cold dawn on the way to an airport to speak in some far-off town the virus is at its lowest point: To hell with it! thinks the patient, almost cured.

Also, I wanted to get an impression of character. I have often thought and written that if the United States were ever to have a Caesar, a true subverter of the state, (1) he would attract to himself all the true believers, the extremists, the hot-eyed custodians of the Truth; (2) he would oversimplify some difficult but vital issue, putting himself on the side of the majority, as Huey Long did when he proclaimed every man a king and proposed to divvy up the wealth; (3) he

would not in the least resemble the folk idea of a dicta-
tor. He would not be an hysteric like Hitler. Rather, he
would be just plain folks, Will Rogers or Arthur Godfrey, a regular guy, warm and sincere, and while he
was amusing us on television the Storm Troopers would
gather in the streets.

Now I have put the case extremely only because in
recent months there has been an unusual rash of extremist groups like the John Birch Society, reminding
us that there is a totalitarian potential in this country
just as there is in every country. Fortunately, barring
military or economic disaster, none of these groups
is apt to come to much without a leader who could appeal personally and irrelevantly to a majority because
of his personal magnetism. It seemed to me that Goldwater was perhaps such a man: (1) He has already attracted many extremists, and he has not denied them;
(2) he oversimplifies a great many issues (getting
"tough" with the Russians is fine and getting rid of the
income tax is fine, too, but toughness costs money;
where will it come from?); (3) he is exactly the sort of
charming man whom no one would suspect of Caesar-
ism, least of all himself.

Barry Goldwater entered Mrs. Coerver's office in his
shirt sleeves and said, "Come on in." At the door to his
own office he turned to a departing interviewer and
said, finishing some earlier thought: "You know, of all
the untrue things they write, the wildest one is how
I'm a millionaire. I've been called that now so many

23

times I'm beginning to feel like I ought to live like one."
Chuckling at his own hyperbole (he is a millionaire;
he does live like one), he led me into his office. The
large desk was catercornered so that the light from the
windows was in the visitor's face. Beside the desk was
a bookcase containing, among other works, a leatherbound set of the speeches of Barry Goldwater. On the
mantel of the fireplace was a bust of Lincoln. In the
far corner of the room stood three flags. One of them
was the Senator's own flag: he is a brigadier general in
the Air Force Reserve. On the walls were photographs
of the Arizona landscape, as beautiful and empty as a
country of the moon.

We sat and looked at each other a moment. At fifty-
two, he is lean and obviously in fine condition. The hair
is gray. The eyes are alert, dark and small; the face
tanned from a recent trip home. The nose is pleasantly
crooked. The nostrils are odd, visible only when he tilts
his head back, like the small neatly round punctures
in a child's rubber mask. The mouth is wide and thin-
lipped, the jaw square. The smile is attractive but
when his face is in repose there is an unexpected hardness, even harshness. Neither of us, I noticed, was very
good at looking straight at the other. Simultaneously,
each looked away. I looked out the window. Goldwater examined his brigadier general's flag (for those
who believe the old saw that an honest man must
have a direct gaze, I refer them to a contemporary's

report that the shiftiest-eyed man he had ever met was Thomas Jefferson).

I began compassionately: "You must get awfully tired of being interviewed." He smiled. "It's repetitive, but . . ." His voice trailed off. It is a good voice for politics, light but earnest, with a slight rural accent of the sort made familiar by television Westerns.

I had debated whether to bring a tape recorder. I knew that Goldwater had a small wrist-watch recorder which he used gleefully to disconcert others as well as to protect himself from misquotation. I decided to take notes instead. On a small pad of paper I had written a few topics. First, the John Birch Society. Recently Goldwater had said that "a great many fine people" were members, including "Republicans, liberal Democrats, conservatives," and he thought it would cause considerable political embarrassment if they were attacked en masse. He had also implied that besides the two known Birchers in Congress, Representatives Edgar Hiestand and John Rousselot, both Republicans of California, there were others. In one interview, however, he suggested that Robert Welch resign. Later he denied he had said this. I asked him how well he knew Welch. He frowned thoughtfully.

"Well, I've known Bob Welch five, maybe six years. But I didn't really get to him until that summit business, you know, when we all tried to keep Eisenhower from meeting Khrushchev. Welch and I worked to-

gether then. Of course all that stuff of his about Eisenhower being a Communist and so on was silly. Fact,
I told him when he gave me that book of his [*The
Politician*] to read, I said: 'Unless you can prove every
one of those statements about people being Communists
is true, you better go destroy every single copy of that
book.'"

"Do you think Welch should resign as head of the
society?"

The answer was quick: "I do. Just the other day I sent
somebody over to the Library of Congress to get me
the bylaws of the Birch Society, and I was disturbed
about this dictatorial thing, how he personally can
chuck people out any time he pleases. I didn't like it."

"What did you mean when you said there were
liberal Democrats in the Birch Society?"

"Because there are. There're all kinds of people in
that group. I know. I've met 'em and a nicer-looking
bunch you never saw. That thirty- to forty-five-year-old
group you want in politics. They're thoughtful people
and they're concerned. But don't get the idea they're
all conservatives because they're fighting Communism.
A lot of people are fighting Communism who aren't
conservative." I had the impression he wanted it made
clear that his own conservative position was one thing
and the fight against Communism was another thing.
Most conservatives regard the two as synonymous. Goldwater does ordinarily, but this day I felt he was prepar-
ing a possible escape hatch.

26

I asked him if he knew of any members of Congress who belonged to the society, other than the two Californians. He paused. Then he said, "No." It was a slow, thoughtful "no," hard to interpret. Then: "You know, I don't really know that much about those people."

I asked him if he approved of their methods, as outlined in Welch's *Blue Book.* "Never read it. I don't know." It seemed to me strange that he would read the bylaws and *The Politician* yet not read the *Blue Book,* which contains not only the bylaws but a ten-point program on how to expose and discourage "Communists."

I mentioned some of Welch's gambits: infiltrating school boards and library boards, getting "mean and dirty" with known liberals, encouraging students to spy on teachers.

Goldwater interrupted. No, he didn't like that, of course. "In fact, I've always been in favor of teaching Communism in schools. Show the kids what we're up against. Naturally I'd want a good course in American history to balance it. After all, the only way you're going to beat Communism is with a better idea, like Nero and the Christians . . . you know? He couldn't stamp 'em out, because there was that idea they had. Well, that's what we've got to have."

Goldwater had been against Federal aid to education. First, he is not convinced any aid is needed. Second, he feels that to give money to the states is an invasion of states' rights. Recently he testified before a

House Education subcommittee in the interests of a bill of his own which he said would solve the whole problem. He proposed giving property owners a rebate on their Federal income tax up to one hundred dollars, the amount to represent what the property owner had paid in local school taxes. Even Goldwater's admirers found this solution baffling. His exchange with Representative John Brademas in committee had a good deal of unconscious humor in it.

Brademas asked Goldwater why he had proposed a bill to answer a problem which he did not believe existed. Soon both men were lost in a maze of: "I said 'if.' Well, if there is a problem, which I don't believe, then here's the answer. . . . All right, but if there is *not* a problem, then why propose . . .?"

In the course of his testimony, Goldwater unexpectedly came out for minimum academic standards to be set by the Federal government for the entire country. Brademas pointed out the contradiction: to set such standards and requirements would mean government intervention of the most extreme sort. Goldwater saw no contradiction: the government's minimum standards would not be compulsory; they would be "guide lines." He felt, too, that although Federal aid to education was unconstitutional, *if* there was to be such aid parochial and private schools should be included.

I teased Goldwater about his exchange with Brademas. He laughed. He then repeated his position: There was no problem, and it was growing less. He quoted statistics. . . . Neither of us listened. I had touched a familiar button. He was responding as he had many times before.

I was amused during the Nixon–Kennedy debates by those who were astonished at the wide range of knowledge displayed by the two men, at their mastery of detail. Actually, neither was asked a question he had not already answered on an average of a dozen times a day for months. After such rehearsal any politician can discuss a number of subjects with what seems encyclopedic detail. It is a trick of the trade but a dangerous one, for answering the same questions over and over interferes with thought. Goldwater finished his statistics and waited for me to press the next button.

Not wanting to get him on a familiar track, I thought quickly, a little desperately. I wanted a general subject. The idea of the Presidency occurred to me. What would *he* do if he were President? Goldwater had once said to a journalist that, all in all, he preferred the Senate to the White House because as a Senator he could speak his mind, "where if you're President you can't. You got to be cautious and watch what you say." When the journalist asked Goldwater what he had been saying as a Senator that he would not feel free to say as President, he had looked baffled and finally said, "Well, damned if I know."

On the word "President" I noticed a faint flush of the fever. His eyes glittered. He sat back in his chair.

"If I was President," he began with a new weight and authority, "I'd move slowly, cautiously at first. You'd have to feel your pathway. Not that my ideas are new ideas. No, they're old, old ideas."

Then he talked of government farm supports. In the campaign, he had demanded "prompt and final termination of all subsidy." But he has changed. He would still eliminate supports, but gradually. I mentioned that only about half of the nation's farmers are needed to grow most of our food. Without supports a lot of people would be thrown on the labor market — in addition to the five million already unemployed. This, I suggested, was a real crisis. He agreed. They would have to be absorbed gradually. But how? Well, management and labor would get together (*without* the government) and set up a joint program to retrain and reallocate displaced people, "Not just farmers either, anybody who's been displaced by mechanization, and so on," and to sponsor "basic research for new gadgets — you know, for a lot of things like that we need."

Could labor and management be relied upon to do the job without some urging from the government? He thought they could. "Of course back in the 1920's management was pretty stupid, but I think they've come of age now, lot of fine new people at the top. The day of those self-made men, the founders, all that's over. In fact, labor's at the same place today management was in the 1920's. All those labor leaders, they're the same type of self-made man ran big business in the old days."

I asked him about his quarrel with Reuther. ("I would rather have Jimmy Hoffa stealing my money than Walter Reuther stealing my freedom.") He shook his head. "It's not personal. I just don't believe labor should be in politics." I was about to ask him what he thought of management in politics (the N.A.M., the Chamber of Commerce) when we were interrupted. A visiting lawyer was outside. He would like to shake the Senator's hand. He was ushered in.

The lawyer was a pleasant-looking, somewhat tense young man who was in Washington for the American Bar Association's antitrust conference. Goldwater came around from behind his desk. He smiled warmly. They shook hands. The young lawyer said in a voice shaking with emotion, "I just wanted you to know, Senator, there are a lot of people over in that Justice Department who better get off their fud and realize we've got some states that can do the job." Goldwater was sympathetic. I turned away, embarrassed. Two conservatives had met and I felt their intensity, their oneness. They spoke in their own shorthand and they knew the enemy.

I made notes while they talked. I wondered idly if I should ask Goldwater what he liked to eat and whether or not he wore pajamas and if he liked movies. I have always enjoyed reading those interviews which are made up of an incredible amount of minutiae; like coral islands they rise bit by bit out of the sea of personality, formed of dead facts. Absently, with what I hoped was the eye of a naturalist-novelist, I began to record the objects on his desk: a large transparent plastic duck mysteriously containing a small metal elephant, all mounted rather disagreeably on a penholder. Next to the duck was a clipping from a Hartford newspaper whose editorial began, *Well, What About Goldwater?* On the wall behind the desk hung a number of small photographs. There was one of Nixon, smiling, with a long inscription which I was too far away to read, There was a similar photograph of Eisenhower, also smiling, also inscribed. Why are politicians so happy when on view? "Always smiling," I wrote neatly on the pad. Then the young lawyer shook hands again. Goldwater smiled. I smiled. The photographs smiled. Only the young lawyer did not smile. He knew the Republic was in danger. He left. Goldwater and I put our smiles away and resumed the interview.

I had been told that the one question which made him uncharacteristically edgy was: Who wrote his book, *The Conscience of a Conservative?* I asked it. He frowned. "That's what wrote it," he said, somewhat irrelevantly. He ran his hand across the row of leatherbound books. "My speeches. The book's nothing but a selection from speeches, from a lot of the things I've been saying for years. After all, I've written four books, a lot of magazine articles, my column."

I had been told that among his literary ghosts were Steve Shadegg and L. Brent Bozell. I started to ask him about them but decided not to. It was cruel. It was pointless. We live in an age of ghosts: singers whose high notes are ghosted by others; writers whose works are created by editors; actors whose performances are made out of film by directors. Why should one harry politicians for not writing their own books and speeches? Few have the time or the talent. In any case the work published must necessarily reflect the views of its "author."

I was ready to drop the subject, but Goldwater was not. He told me he was planning another book. He was going on a cruise with his wife in the fall. While traveling, he would write the first draft. Then he would go over it carefully for "improvement in expression. Then after that I'll submit it to an author . . . I mean publisher." I suspect that Goldwater knows even less about Freud than I do, which is little, but we both know a Freudian slip when we hear one. The dark eyes darted anxiously in my direction. Had I caught the slip? I had.

He talked about conservatism. "Bunch of us got together after the convention and we all agreed we'd never heard such conservative speeches get so much applause, and then they go and accept that platform which 95 per cent of them were against." He sighed. "I don't know. What's wrong with the word 'conservative' anyway? Must be something." He said he had been impressed by the British Conservatives' comeback in 1951. They had got out and sold the party to the young people. This was his own plan. He would sell conservatism wherever he could, preferably to the young and uncommitted. "Of course the Conservative Party in England is about like the New Deal was here."

I asked him his impression of Kennedy. "Well, I guess I know him about as well as anybody around here. I like him. Of course we disagree on a lot of things. He thinks the government should do a lot more for people than I do." He mused about the campaign. He had advised against Nixon's television debates with Kennedy. "Funny, when my sister saw the first one, she said, 'Why, that Kennedy isn't so young!' And I knew then and there that was it. Of course, on sheer debating points Nixon took Kennedy every time. Anybody who knows about these things could see that. Especially on Quemoy and Matsu. Boy, if *I* had been debating Kennedy, I sure would have jazzed him all over the lot — Berlin, Laos, everything!"

I commented that Nixon had been a victim of his own legend. He had been pictured by both admirers and enemies as a rough infighter, a merciless debater, a ruthless killer, yet in the campaign and in the television debates it was quite clear that of the two, Kennedy was by far the tougher fighter. Goldwater nodded. "I warned Nixon about that a long time ago when the real mistake was made, 'way back there in California in that Senate election. You see, Nixon was sold by these people on putting himself over as a real gut fighter. They figured it would do him good against Helen Gahagan Douglas. So they built him up tough and mean, when of course he wasn't, when all he ever did was just tell the truth about that woman. The whole thing about him being so mean was nothing but publicity. So I told him: 'You wait and see, when you get to running for President and you start getting rough, the way you *got* to, they'll jump on you and say it's the old Nixon.' And they did. And then he'd pussyfoot." Goldwater shook his head sadly.

We talked about medical care for the aged to be paid through Social Security. The Senator was against it. He said that at the Arizona hospital of which he was a director, only one elderly person had been unable to pay. He had also seen a poll from western Florida where the elderly people had voted firmly against Federal aid. I suggested that those who could afford to retire to Arizona and Florida might be comfortably off. He said no, their average income was about $300 a month. Anyway, people ought to look after themselves either through their own foresight or through help from their families. Failing that, indigence should be handled the way it has always been: at the local level, by charities and so on.

I suggested that with taxes as high as they are, and longer life expectancies, there would be more rather than fewer programs for state and Federal aid in the coming years. He agreed. That was why he felt the whole tax structure had to be overhauled. And though he no longer favors repealing the graduated income tax, as he suggested in his book, he did feel that taxes on business should be reduced and greater allowance made for depreciation. "I told Jack Kennedy: you could be President for life if you'd just lift some of those taxes so that businessmen — and I know hundreds of 'em — would have some incentive to get new machinery, to overhaul their plants, to *really* start producing."

Publicly, no American politician can admit that we have anything to learn from the experiments of any other society. The ritual dialogue between office seeker and electorate is one of mutual congratulation, and to suggest that perfection has another home is treasonable. But privately our more conscientious legislators do ponder other countries' penal reforms, medical programs, educational methods. From his book and speeches I suspected Goldwater had done little or no homework. He was firmly against socialized medicine, but he seemed to know nothing about how it worked in Scandinavia, West Germany, England.

Goldwater was honest. No, he didn't know much about European socialism. "But I did meet this Norwegian doctor, matter of fact her name was Goldwater, which is how she happened to get in touch with me. She said the thing *seemed* to work all right, but that being assured of a certain income every month from the government kept her from feeling any real urge to study harder — you know, keep up at her profession. There was no incentive." I asked him if he thought that the desire to be good was entirely economic in origin. He said of course it was. I then asked him to explain how it was that two people as different as ourselves worked hard, though in neither case was money the spur. He was startled. Then he murmured vaguely and slipped away from the subject.

I asked him what he felt about some of his more odd-ball admirers. Goldwater became suddenly cautious. The quick, easy responses were replaced by a slow, careful measuring of words. He knew, he said, of some 250 organizations either conservative or anti-Communist. He admitted it was often difficult to figure out who was what. "Every invitation I get to speak, I have to check it for this and check it for that, make absolutely sure they're O.K. You never know what you may be getting into. Some are first-rate, like this fellow in New Orleans, Ken Courtney. He publishes a magazine down there. He's quite a guy." He asked on the phone for the magazine's name. I mentioned the Young Americans for Freedom, an organization founded by those who had been involved in the Youth for Goldwater movement at the Chicago convention. He approved of them highly, especially of "What's his name — Gaddy? Caddy, that's right. Nice kid, a real savvy guy with a lot on the ball."

Mrs. Coerver entered. "The magazine's called *Independent American,* and his name is Kent, not Ken, Courtney." She left.

More than once, Goldwater has complained that though the Republican Party's leaders are conservative they invariably choose liberal or moderate candidates to run for President on the false (to him) premise that a true conservative could never win. I asked him, Why not start a third party?

Goldwater sat up briskly. "If I thought it would work, I might. But I don't know . . . third parties never get off the ground in this country. There was Teddy Roosevelt, and there was . . ." He shook his head. "No, I don't see it. For one thing, conservatism is pretty divided. Suppose I started a party. Then somebody would come along and say, 'Well, look here, you're not *my* kind of conservative,' and then he'd go off and start *his* party and you'd end up like France. That's the trouble with the conservatives. They've got this all-or-nothing attitude." He sighed. "Why, I got booed in New York when I said if it was between Rockefeller and Harriman I'd be for Rockefeller. I tried to explain how at least Rockefeller was a Republican and you got your foot in the door. . . . No. A political party can only start around a strong individual." He looked past me at the bust on the mantelpiece; his jaw had set. "Like Lincoln. The people were there looking for a party, looking for this strong individual. And there he was and that's how the Republican Party started. A strong individual."

The next question was obvious. Was Goldwater that "strong individual"? Could he lead his people out of the wilderness? Were there enough of them to allow him to re-create that dream of Eden which conservatives evoke whenever they recall the bright simple days of our old agrarian Republic? But I let it go. Neither of us knew the answer. He had his hopes, and that was enough.

I rose to go. He walked me to the door. We exchanged impieties, each about his own political party, then said good-by.

"Ignorant but shrewd" was the verdict of one colleague of Goldwater. "He's read very little. He has no knowledge of economics. He's completely outside the world of ideas. Even his passion for the Constitution is based upon a misunderstanding of its nature." I am not sure I would agree that Goldwater's ignorance of ideas is necessarily relevant to his ability or his capacity for growth.

I was impressed by his charm, which, even for a politician, is considerable. More than that, in his simplifying of great issues Goldwater has a real appeal for a nation which is not at all certain about its future either as a society or as a world power. Up and down the land there are storm warnings. Many look nervously for shelter, and Goldwater, in the name of old-time virtue and ruggedness and self-reliance, offers them refuge beneath the venerable great roof of the Constitution. True or not, his simplifications are enormously appealing and, who knows, in a time of crisis he might seize the prize.

But I make no predictions. I would only recommend to Goldwater Cicero's warning to a fellow political adventurer, in a falling year of the Roman Republic: "I am sure you understand the political situation into which you have . . . no, not stumbled, but stepped; for it was by deliberate choice and by no accident that you flung your tribunate into the very crisis of things; and I doubt not that you reflect how potent in politics is opportunity, how shifting the phases, how incalculable the issues of events, how easily swayed are men's predilections, what pitfalls there are and what insincerity in life." *

[*Life,* June 9, 1961.]

* See Note 2 in the Appendix.

THE HOUSE UN-AMERICAN
ACTIVITIES COMMITTEE

WHEN I WAS RUNNING for Congress last year (now there's a phrase to empty a room!) I was asked the same planted question at nearly every meeting: Are you in favor of the House Un-American Activities Committee? My answer was usually more cautious than candid. For purposes of legislation, Congress has a constitutional right to investigate anything it wants to, and I am all for Congress's traditional privilege, but then I would suggest tactfully to my audience that HUAC had produced less legislation at a greater cost than any committee in Congressional history, and as for its chairmen . . . Well, who could admire Martin Dies? Or that superpatriot J. Parnell Thomas, who went from Congress to the clink? Or the present chairman, Francis Walter, whose only legislative distinction is the notori-

4 1

ous McCarran-Walter Immigration Act, a sly bit of work Cardinal Cushing felt could not "be defended without recourse to the discredited and un-Christian tenet of racism." I left the subject there, realizing that the lunatic Right has worked out a fine (and to many people perfectly reasonable) syllogism. HUAC is against un-American activities. Mr. Blank is against HUAC. Therefore, Mr. Blank *favors* un-American activities.

Fortunately, a brilliant case against HUAC has now been made by Frank J. Donner, a constitutional lawyer, in a book called *The Unamericans.* Using transcripts and documents, Donner records the whole sordid history of HUAC from its beginning in 1938. Originally, HUAC was a short-term investigating committee which evolved gradually into a standing committee, though, contrary to precedent, its function is not legislative, but simply "exposing" Communists. John Rankin of Mississippi was godfather to HUAC in the House at the time of its metamorphosis in 1945. When Walter Winchell, among others, attacked the committee, Rankin dismissed the columnist with characteristic charm as "that Communistic little kike."

Neither in the past nor in the present has HUAC ever found un-American any fascist or racist organization. In fact, in 1942, the Ku Klux Klan's Imperial Wizard James Colescott said, "The committee's program so closely parallels the program of the Klan that there's no distinguishable difference between them." As for the John Birch Society, Gordon Scherer, HUAC's ranking

Republican member, is one of that society's "Sponsors." Not only is the committee instinctive in its dislike of the foreign-born and colored minorities, it is even on record as opposing "racial and social equality."

The final irony, of course, is that as the Communist menace outside the United States increases, inside it decreases (today there are about twenty thousand American Communists, a small fraction of what there was in the 1940's). Yet the hate groups grow more hysterical every day in their search for "Communists." Actually, their real targets are liberals, minority groups, intellectuals, "do-gooders." (They themselves are proud "do-badders.") Their method is now so odd that if someone they dislike actively fights Communists (e.g., Dean Acheson), they will say: But that's his plot; he only *seems* to fight Communists; he's really a spy. . . . This way paranoia — and Candy Man Bob Welch, the Big Bircher — lies. Fortunately, we now have Mr. Donner's book, and I'm certain anyone who reads it will agree with Harry Truman that "the most un-American thing in America is the House Un-American Activities Committee."

[*New York Herald Tribune,* July 14, 1961.]

43

HUAC REVISITED

"I AN," I said, "are you, or were you ever, a Communist?" Ian Ballantine, a short reddish man (in physical coloring only, let me add quickly) with heavily tufted eyebrows, shook his head, knit the tufted brows, and roared "No!" I turned to Frank Donner, whom I had just met, and asked him the same question. No, he was not a Communist now, but he had been a party member during the Forties. I was both exhilarated and alarmed: it was just like those grand days back in the Fifties when Tail-gunner Joe fired at will and the smell of heretics burning was sharp upon the air. Now, in 1961, we three sat in the bar of the Plaza Hotel in New York, questioning one another's loyalty. It was thrilling.

What was the occasion? Ian Ballantine is the publisher of Ballantine Books, a paperback house most noted for its science fiction. Recently, the firm has

begun publishing books of topical political comment.
I have known Ian Ballantine for seven years (already
this is beginning to sound like testimony); he has
reprinted two of my novels. I would put a great
deal of money on his loyalty to Old Glory. A few
months ago he published a book by Frank Donner
called *The Unamericans*—a well-documented exposé
of the House Un-American Activities Committee, one
of the less savory heirlooms of the Thirties still to haunt
the national attic. Ballantine sent me the book to read.
I was impressed — and horrified — by it. When John
Crosby of the *New York Herald Tribune* went on vaca-
tion in the summer, he asked me to write a column for
him. I wrote about *The Unamericans*. Well, sir, the Radical Right really hit the fan.

The counterattack began. From ultra-foolish Fulton
Lewis Jr. to the Committee's chairman, Francis Walter,
the attack was suspiciously the same. The book should
be completely discredited because Donner had been
a Communist. None of the charges made against HUAC
were answered. The smear-tactic, second nature to
these patriots, is always the same: get your critic on
some other ground; never answer a charge; never defend, *attack!* In the House of Representatives, Francis
Walter attacked Donner. Gordon Scherer attacked me.
I will quote some of Scherer's speech for appreciation
of the style, as Stendhal would say. (*Note to HUAC:*
Stendhal was a radical French writer, now deceased.
I will not conceal the fact that his real name was Henri

Beyle. *Note to readers:* The Committee once threatened to investigate Christopher Marlowe.) After calling me a "left-wing writer" — I who am solidly "wing" — Scherer congratulated the discerning voters of my district for having spared the House the onus of my membership in it. Then he went on to say: "A few weeks ago in *Life*, Vidal did a subtle and clever smear-job upon the junior Senator from Arizona." (A real tribute, by the way; most of the patriots thought I was "obvious" and "heavy-handed.") "In the *Herald Tribune* of last week he did a vicious and not-so-subtle smear-job on the Committee on Un-American Activities . . . to build up the book, he refers to the author, Frank Donner, as a brilliant constitutional lawyer. He conceals the fact that Donner was an underground Communist while employed by the Government of the U.S. . . ."

Now let us pause and savor the style. I have been accused, if you notice, of "concealing" a relevant fact. But I did not know that Donner had been a Communist. It is not usual, when reviewing a book, to request a dossier on the author. But most of Donner's charges against the Committee were familiar to me, as they were to Harry Truman, the *New York Times,* Bishop Pike and all the other hostile critics of the Committee. What I admired about Donner's indictment was the thorough presentation of testimony.

Then Scherer says: "Vidal further concealed the fact that Bertram Edises assisted Donner in the preparation of the book. Edises' whole record of service to the Communist cause is set forth on page 36 of the Committee's report entitled 'Communist Legal Subversion.'" Notice again the style: *Vidal "concealed."* The patriots live in a world of conspiracy and threat. Scherer would give the impression that I was holding back information in a malicious attempt to mislead. But I did not know Edises had assisted Donner. Like most readers, I tend to skip the acknowledgments at the beginnings of books: the To-My-Wife-Without-Whose-Invaluable-Assistance kind of thing. But if I *had* read it, I would have been no wiser. Edises, regardless of the excitement he causes in Scherer's sturdy breast, is a demonstrably obscure American. Yet from what I have since been able to find out about him, though he displeases the Committee, he seemed not to be a Communist. But if he is a Communist, wouldn't Donner himself have tried to conceal the fact of his assistance?

To continue with Scherer: "If Gore Vidal had been interested in the truth, as he apparently was in rehabilitating the Communist Party and its members, he would have reviewed the Committee reports on the Axis front movement based on 288 organizations. . . ." Scherer then gives his only defense of the Committee. He denies that HUAC has been soft on fascist groups — a somewhat sensitive area for a man known to be a sponsor of the John Birch Society. Yet evidence of HUAC's softness toward racist-fascist groups is well known. In fact, in 1941 Representative Samuel Dickstein, who was responsible for the 1934 resolution authorizing a House investigation of subversive activities, surveying the monster he had created, said: "One hundred ten fascist organizations in the United States have had and have now the key to the back door of the Un-American Activities Committee."

While Scherer was attacking me, Walter was chattering shrilly about Donner's past. Over and over again, he claimed that (*a*) Donner had been a Communist and (*b*) therefore the book was not true. Of course (*b*) does not necessarily follow from (*a*). Donner's charges remain unanswered. Also, he is not a Communist now, as far as anyone knows, but if he should be a Soviet agent, then the F.B.I. ought to arrest him; otherwise, he is a free citizen in a free country. In any case, Walter's irrelevancy would be thrown out of a court of law. It is as if a man were to witness a terrible automobile accident, only to find that his testimony was inadmissible because he had, ten years before, been booked for speeding. Walter also said he was reluctant to mention the book at all because "I have no desire to swell the coffers of the Communist Party by stimulating its sale." Of course Congressmen are protected from slander suits by the Constitution but if such a remark were made *outside* the immunity of the House, it would be well worth slapping a suit on Walter, for he would have to prove that both Donner and Ballantine had given the Communist Party money from the sale of this book. But this sort of slack-mouthed chatter is mischievous. "Oh, yes, Ballantine's a Communist. Didn't you see where he gave money to the Communist Party? It's all there in the *Congressional Record*." And the melon-heads will nod raptly: "Yep, that's right. There it is in black and white. Must be true."

I shall not score Scherer other than to say that he is as beautifully fatuous a creature as ever swung down out of the tangled trees of American politics. Happily, not long ago he got his come-uppance from that sharp-tongued septuagenarian Senator Stephen Young of Ohio. In 1959 when Young was announced as a speaker before the Emergency Civil Liberties Union in New York, Scherer thundered: "I don't see how any real American who is aware of the Communist domination of the ECLU can connect himself with it in any capacity." To which the testy Senator replied: "Gordon H. Scherer, in my opinion, misrepresents the First Ohio Congressional District. It would be a good thing for Ohio if the voters catch up with him and defeat him next November. This self-proclaimed patriot never wore the uniform of his country in time of war. He enjoyed a safe-salaried position as Safety Director of Cincinnati while millions of us were overseas in combat." A salvo of praise for Senator Young sounded in the press. His enemy took to the woods.

Scherer has been evasive, to say the least, about his connection with the John Birch Society. He has been listed as a Sponsor. Yet word has got around that he is not in accord with that despotic group. To date he has not made a straight statement one way or the other. If he *has* changed his mind about the Birchers, I for one would welcome him home to the free world. Like his committee, if there is one thing I prefer to an informer, it's a turncoat. Certainly, he owes his fans an explanation: does he or does he not believe along with Big Bircher Bob Welch, the Candy Man of Belmont, Mass., that Dwight Eisenhower and forty million Americans are Communists? If he does not, all he need do is to recant and demonstrate his friendliness to the nation by naming the names of all his Birch Society associates. Otherwise, we must hold him in contempt.

I may as well confess that I was secretly delighted at being identified as "a leftist writer," "apparently" trying to rehabilitate the Communist Party. In actual fact, I have always been a conservative cross borne sadly by liberal friends. I began life as an absolute monarchist, on condition of course that *I* be that monarch. At about fifteen, I shifted reluctantly to the idea of constitutional monarchy, privately deploring the fact that George Washington had not become king. By seventeen, I had got around to the American Constitution and, for all its flaws, I have yet to see for us a better alternative to our form of government.

Temperamentally, I am suspicious of belonging to anything. When I ran for office, I debated seriously whether or not to run as an Independent, because I was not eager to be saddled with the Democratic Party

— on the ground that *any* party label is committing. But I compromised and became a Democrat. Then, since I favored Federal aid to education, medical care for the aged, the Bill of Rights, and so on, an attempt was made, as is now standard in American politics, to say that I was a Communist (there are, by the way, some 20,000 Communists in America, according to J. Edgar Hoover). Much research was done into my past. To the consternation of the enemy it was found that I had never joined *anything* . . . almost.

Patriots, I have a confession to make. So far, your committee has not found out my secret. Even so, after twenty-one years of guilt, I am willing to sing. In 1940, at the Phillips Exeter Academy, when I was fourteen years old, I joined the America First Committee. There, I've said it. A mountain is lifted off my conscience. I was a dedicated Anglophobe and isolationist. I was reluctant to help England "get her chestnuts out of the fire." (Remember?) I organized a school group to fight "Bundles for Britain" and those other interventionist groups we called (and I blush at the memory) Communist! Not until I entered the Army at seventeen did I cease to be an isolationist. I give two reasons for my early position. One: the influence of my grandfather, a Senator of great wit and charm who had been a Populist and, like most Western radicals of that era, profoundly isolationist. The other reason is more serious and worthy of investigation. During those years, I ate a great many Welch Fudge Bars. They were distributed mostly in New England, the product of . . . yes, you've guessed it: Big Bircher Robert Welch himself. There was something in those delicious fudge bars which was reactionary. I have since checked with fellow schoolmates who were also extremely right-wing in those days and, to a man, I found that they, too, had been addicted to Welch Fudge Bars. Yet each, when he left New England and was no longer able to get his quota of this particular candy, became liberal. Now I'm not making any accusations. I don't want to invoke the Pure Food and Drug Act, just yet. All I say is that it's a funny coincidence, and, as Tail-gunner Joe used to say, *it looks like part of a pattern*.

Both Donner and Ballantine have felt the wrath of the Radical Right since *The Unamericans* was published. Donner receives many threatening telephone calls. One anonymous caller said: "Donner, I give you warning; by tonight you and your family will be wiped out." I also read some of his mail and it is fine sick stuff, often with a Texas or Arizona postmark.

Harassment of Ballantine has been even more interesting. After the book was published, the Committee promptly sent one of its investigators to his firm's bank to warn them that Ballantine not only publishes but employs Communists. Ultra-foolish Fulton Lewis Jr. (whose son works for the Committee) attacked Ballantine in one of his columns, pointing out that one of his employees had taken the Fifth Amendment before the Committee. That, it seems, is enough. Employ

a "Fifth Amendment Communist," and you yourself
are guilty by association. This lunacy was carried to its
extreme by the Committee's counsel when he denounced Eisenhower as un-American for allowing his
grandchildren to meet Khrushchev. The Committee's
harassment, down the years, of Ballantine's employee
is a remarkable horror story and should one day be
written.

For those who may not be able to accept Donner's
book because of his past, I would suggest that they read
Telford Taylor's *Grand Inquest* (Ballantine). It is a
scholarly account of Congressional investigation from
sixteenth-century British parliamentary origins to the
present. Taylor's comments about HUAC are quite as
devastating as Donner's. And let me add quickly that
despite all efforts to smear him, Mr. Taylor not only
has never been a Communist but is one of the most
famous of American lawyers. He was Chief Counsel for
the Prosecution at the Nuremberg Trials. More to the
point, he was himself a Congressional investigator
(1935-1939). His credentials are in order, though one
can hear the gibbons chattering in the trees: "How *can*
you believe Telford Taylor? Didn't you know his publisher employs an art director who once took the Fifth
Amendment?" The melonheads would look very grave
at that.

The constitutional case against HUAC is simply this:
For legislative purposes, Congress has the power to
investigate anything it chooses. But the operative phrase

is "legislative purposes." The Congress is not a court. It may not "expose" for the sake of exposing. It may not condemn or judge anyone. As Thomas Jefferson put it, after one of his own wars with the House: "I observed here a difference between the British Parliament and our Congress, that the former was a legislature, an inquest for the King. The latter was by the Constitution, a legislature and an inquest, *but not a council.*" From its inception, HUAC has created almost no legislation. It has been devoted to "exposing" Communists. For what purpose? Partly for the sake of publicity for Committee members and partly to make mischief for those exposed (usually, liberals politically opposed to the Right Wing). Had the Committee addressed itself to finding subversives in government and other sensitive areas, it might have been able to maintain some semblance of seriousness — though, even then, it would not be serving any legislative function. But what is one to make of the strange lists of people who are called before it? One day, in Washington, HUAC summoned a doctor, an optometrist, a commerical artist, a magazine writer, an electrician, an automobile mechanic, a piano tuner, a public relations consultant, a commercial photographer and two housewives. Not one of these people was working in an area where he could do harm to the nation. Why call them? To get more names, the Committee would answer. What would be done with those names? Call the new names, too, and ask them if they were ever Communists and, if so, to give more names of associates. Why? The same thing, on and on forever. Yet the Committee is not a court. It cannot try these people. Nor is it a law enforcement body. Yet the melonheads have been falsely led to believe that the Committee is finding spies and Soviet agents. But it is not; it cannot. Under the Constitution, the Committee can only gather information with an eye to legislation. What legislation comes out of these quizzes? In any case, espionage statutes are on the books already. Yet if more legislation *were* needed, espionage, subversion and sabotage come under the staid, useful House Judiciary Committee, not HUAC. As for spy-catching, that is the task of the F.B.I., not members of Congress.

Ordinarily, if the Committee were remotely responsible, there would be nothing wrong with talking to a lot of people who may or may not have been involved in the Communist Party in the Thirties and Forties. A dialogue conducted sincerely would be educational for all of us. But what has proved vicious is the Committee's insistence on naming names. Most witnesses have been willing to co-operate as far as confessing their own political sins. But many refuse to turn informer. That is when they take the Fifth Amendment. For a long time our society was based upon a certain attitude of trust held between citizens. You didn't tattle in school; you didn't rat in adulthood. I think that is a good trait. The Committee, like its Soviet counterparts, thinks otherwise, putting informing, next to recanting, as the highest virtue. If one has been "unfriendly" to the Committee, efforts will be made to get the witness fired from his job, while his bank, neighbors and school district will be informed that he has been "unfriendly" to the Committee. In nearly every case, the victim is ostracized: a new form of treatment in our society, comparable to that of the Soviet, where, nowadays, heretics are not imprisoned but made literally, *out*laws — the late Boris Pasternak being the most celebrated victim.

I have gone into considerable detail about all this because, as the pressures upon us increase from the Communist world, there will be more and more signs of stress and strain within the country. Beneath the flat rocks of the Republic lurk odd grubs, worms and scorpions, ready to poison the body politic. In times of crisis the earth rumbles; stones are dislodged and the ugly ones are loose for a time to do damage. In the last year, the rocks have shifted drastically. The Scherers and Welches are loose among us. They exploit legitimate fears to private ends. There is evidence, too, that the Radical Right is now trying to unite itself in order (I put this with exquisite tact) to change our "democracy" into their "republic." I suggest we help them fail.

[*Esquire*, December 1961.]

CLOSING THE CIVILIZATION GAP

FOR SOME TIME NOW our leaders, both demagogic and honest, have been telling us to rouse ourselves to greater purpose, national and private. Walter Lippmann suggests that the United States behaves like a society which thinks it is complete, with no more to accomplish; that, for better or worse, we are what we are, and the only danger to our comfort is external. President Kennedy's exhortations to self-sacrifice are becoming ever more urgent, even shrill. Yet his critics point out that he has not done much to show us how we might best serve our society. To which the answer of the Administration, at least privately, is that until Americans understand those things that threaten us, both from without and within, any Presidential program demanding the slightest sacrifice would be demolished by Congress and the jingo press. After all, things do look all right if you don't look too carefully, and no one can accuse us of ever looking carefully at an unpleasant sight, whether it is Soviet superiority in space or chronic unemployment at home. Now I don't want to add my voice to the general keening. American society has many virtues which we should never underestimate. By fits and starts, we are attaining a civilization and, barring military accident, we shall certainly attain one before the Soviets. "Be the First into Civilization!" Now *there's* a slogan for the two competitors.

Yet for those who are puzzled at how to respond to Presidential cries for action, vigor and moving-aheadness, I propose that there are certain very practical things we can do in a society that is by no means complete. I might add that those professional patriots who trumpet that this is the new Eden and only traitors would change it or downgrade it are declaring, of course, that the society is closed and therefore decadent and soon to fall. I vote No to "perfection," and Yes to change and survival. Most of us spend too much time solving international problems at cocktail parties, rather than dealing with those things which we might affect and change, the tying up of the loose ends in our own society. There are many of them, ranging from the abolition of capital punishment to school integration. On either of those great matters any citizen can be usefully engaged. He can also be useful in social and moral legislation, where there is much work to be done.

As for civil liberties, anyone who is not vigilant may one day find himself living, if not in a police state, at least in a police city. Now I will tell a horror story which has haunted me for several months, something that, I am told, is common but which I witnessed for the first time, reacting as deeply as the writer in Angus Wilson's novel *Hemlock and After*.

I was in Washington for a few days last spring. At about ten o'clock in the evening of my last day in town, I took a taxicab to the Union Station. It was a mild, drizzly night. Traffic in the side streets near Pennsylvania Avenue was tied up. My cab was stopped in front of the YMCA, a large building a half-block from the Old State Department and two blocks from the White House. The sidewalk was deserted. As we sat there, out of the building marched four men, wearing light raincaps with upturned brims and trench coats. There were two men with them. One was well dressed, perhaps sixty; he wore a white raincoat. The other was young and thin and shabby, and he wore no raincoat. I watched as this odd company moved seven or eight yards along the sidewalk toward the traffic light, which was now red. In front of a deserted shop, the lightcaps stopped and methodically began to beat up the two men with them. I sat there stunned. There had been no provocation. As suddenly and pointlessly as a nightmare, the attack began; and there, right in front of me on the black wet sidewalk, the older man lay as two men kicked him, while the other two shoved the young man into the doorway of the shop and began to beat him across the face.

The cab driver, an old Negro, said, "I hate to see anybody do that to another man. I do." The light was now green, but I told him to wait. I got out and crossed to the nearest lightcap. He was, at the moment, disengaged. He had been working the younger man over and he now stood a few feet away, breathing hard. I asked him who he was and what he was doing. He turned on me and I have never seen such a savage, frightening little face. It was plump, flushed, with popping eyes; the face of a young pig gone berserk. He began to scream at me to get out of there or I'd be arrested. Threats and obscenities poured out of him in one long orgiastic breath. I looked away and saw that the older man was now on his stomach, trying to shield his head from the kicks of the men standing over him. His raincoat was streaked with mud. The younger man was silent, except for the whacking noise his face made when it was struck — first left, then right, like a punching bag. In my hardest voice I said: "You're going to be the one in trouble if you don't tell me who you are." The dark one came over to me at this point; he showed me his detective's badge, and suggested I get lost. Then he returned to his sport. The plump one was now longing (and I do not exaggerate by using a verb of judgment) to get back to the man in the doorway. But before he could, I asked him for his name. He started to curse again, but a look from his companion stopped him. He gave me his name and then with a squeal leaped on the man in the doorway and began hitting him, making, as he did, obscene gasping noises.

I stood there dumbly wondering what to do. Right in front of me, two men were being knocked about by four men who were, quite simply, enjoying their work. I was also witness to the fact that the victims had *not* resisted arrest, which would of course be the police explanation for what had happened. Cravenly, I got back into the cab. I asked my driver if he would be a witness with me. He shook his head sadly. "I don't want no trouble. This is a mighty dirty town."

At Union Station I telephoned the *Washington Post and Times-Herald* and talked to the night editor. I gave him my name. Yes, he knew who I was. Yes, the story interested him. I gave him the detective's name, which I had thought was probably false. He said no, there was such a man. I gave him the cab driver's license number, in case the driver changed his mind. Then the editor asked me what I intended to do about it. I shouted into the receiver, "This is your town. Your scandal. Your newspaper. *You* do something about it, I'm catching a train." He asked if they could use my name. I said of course, and hung up.

And that was the end of it. I have often thought of those two since, wondered who they were and what happened to them. I also brooded over the curious horror of seeing our society at its most vicious two blocks from the White House. It is true, as Sartre once wrote, that the real tragedy in our time is that any of us can be, interchangeably, victim or torturer.

I got back to New York to read that a Southern editor had written an editorial attacking the John Birch Society. In the course of his editorial, he quoted the F.B.I. as saying that the Birchers were "irresponsible." Some hours *before* the editorial was published, two men from the F.B.I. arrived at the editor's office and asked him on what authority he could quote the F.B.I. as terming the Birch Society "irresponsible." The editor's sources were not, as it turned out, reliable. But then the editor, quite naturally, asked how it was that the F.B.I. knew the contents of his editorial before it was published. He got no answer.

Now the point to these two stories is that here is something we *can* do: guard our own liberties. We may not be able to save Laos; but we can, as individuals, keep an eye on local police forces, even if it means, as some have proposed, setting up permanent committees of appeal in every city to hear cases of police brutality, or to consider infractions of our freedom to speak out in the pursuit of what our founders termed happiness — two rights always in danger, not only at the local but at the Federal level.*

[*Esquire*, August 1961.]

* See Note 3 in the Appendix.

THE FUTURE OF CONSERVATISM

THE TERMS "liberal" and "conservative" have no precise meaning in current American politics. Originally, a liberal was one who favored changes and reforms tending toward greater democracy, while a conservative was one who resisted change in order to maintain things the way they are. In that sense, at least, Barry Goldwater is a liberal (he does not want greater democracy but he certainly wants to change the status quo: stop all this "welfarism," for instance), while John Kennedy would be a conservative in that he would retain and not greatly expand the present welfare programs of the Federal government.

Despite the cries of the Radical Right, there is no important liberal movement in the United States. By "liberal" I mean socialist in the sense that most of Western Europe is socialist and at the same time democratic. It has been one of the tragedies of our recent politics that the Radical Right has managed to convince the majority of our people that socialism is the same thing as Communism, which is Soviet foreign policy, which is our enemy. The Soviet *is* our enemy, but socialism is *not* Communism, or necessarily Russian-dominated. More important, and a fact that would come as a great surprise to most of our people, it is possible to have a socialist country (Denmark, for instance) which is also a free society, with a representative government just like our own. The fact that our people don't understand that socialism is the preferred form of government of most of the civilized world, not to mention the new countries of Africa and Asia, makes for much misunderstanding in our dealings not only with the enemy but with our allies and would-be friends.

What then is the division in America? It is, I should say, between conservative and reactionary. John Kennedy is a conservative. Barry Goldwater is a reactionary. A reactionary is one who wishes to reverse an existing state of affairs and to return to a previous condition of society. In the case of Goldwater and his fellow reactionaries the previous condition is the old agrarian America, before the income tax, the industrial revolution, the disturbing responsibilities of being a world power. The program of the reactionaries is largely negative. Get the government out of this and out of that;

don't give Federal aid to the schools; don't extend Social Security in any way; do nothing about the five or six million unemployed; save as much money as possible by cutting out all human services so that the income tax can be gradually eliminated.

The sophisticated reactionary knows exactly what he is doing. He wants complete freedom to get as much money as possible with no interference from the government. The freedom to exploit others is the cornerstone of his philosophy. Goldwater's book *The Conscience of a Conservative* is a hymn to self-interest. The simpler, more instinctive reactionary tends to be puzzled and annoyed by the state of affairs in this country. He sees a vast, impersonal, and not very competent government involved in more and more areas of his life. Each year he pays more money to support this government, and with some justification he is resentful. He reacts: just get rid of those taxes, stop giving money to foreigners, don't help out those deadbeats who aren't smart enough to get a job or take care of themselves, then everything will be all right. But the matter is not that simple. Large countries have large governments, and they do cost too much. But as Justice Holmes said, "Taxes are the price we pay for civilization." It is the quality of that civilization which ought to concern "liberal" as well as "conservative." Humanizing government is going to be the principal task of the next hundred years. The reactionary would prefer to eliminate most government, but that will not happen, and attempts to revive old forms and attitudes will fail.

In a sense, the reactionaries can never win, because clocks go forward, not backward. That "simple" America they dream of (it never existed) will not return. Life is complex. If we are to remain a great power, we will have to spend uncomfortable amounts on armaments and foreign aid. Taxes will remain great. Government will always be large, no matter who is at the White House, Kennedy or Goldwater. The tendency toward socialism is as strong in this country as in any other, though we will have to think of a new way to describe it — Dynamic Constitutionalism, perhaps. The limits that government has set on the power of individuals and groups to exploit others will remain. The people — who are the country — will probably want more services from the country, which is themselves, and they will get those services, again no matter who presides at the White House.

Yet it is the dream of the reactionary to stop the majority cold. The reactionary detests our form of government. One of his favorite arguments is: the United States is a republic, not a democracy. But we are *both* a republic and a democracy. What the reactionary really means to say is that the will of the majority as expressed through elections should be circumvented. That there should be a limit to the franchise. The Right Wing has not yet had the courage to propose that some people be allowed to vote and some kept from voting according, say, to the size of their income but that is what they are after. They mistrust and dislike the majority. Yet our Constitution, which they profess to revere, is quite explicit about the value of the democratic process. In fact, the Constitution begins with the words "We the people," not "We, the special interests," or "We, the well-educated and well-to-do."

In free elections in reasonably serene times, the reactionary has no chance at the polls. But these are not serene times. In the event of some economic or military disaster, I suspect that the reactionary elements in America will come together and in one way or another try to take power. Nor would it, sad to relate, be very difficult for them to impose themselves on the very people they dislike, for we have become a passive, ill-informed, fearful society. A recent analysis of high school students should give aid and comfort to those who dislike the democratic process.

Since 1941, H. H. Remmers of Purdue University has been conducting polls in the high schools of the country. I am indebted to a piece by him and D. H. Radler in the *Scientific American* for their most recent findings. Fifty-seven per cent of our high school students believe that the average citizen is justified in remaining aloof from the "dirty" politics that may exist in his community. Sixty per cent believe police and other groups should have the power to ban or censor books and movies. Forty-one per cent believe that newspapers and magazines should not be allowed to print anything they want. Forty-nine per cent believe that "a large mass of people" are not capable of determining what is and what is not good for them. Fifty-eight per cent believe that the police and the F.B.I. should have the right to give a prisoner the third degree. Forty-six per cent believe that there should *not* be more women in public office. Forty-one per cent believe fascism and communism are the same thing. Thirty-four per cent believe the government should prohibit *some* people from making speeches. Having blithely rejected our system of government and the Bill of Rights, we find the children profoundly anti-intellectual. They think scientists are a bit odd, radically inclined, and not "happy." Forty per cent believe that the earth is the center of the universe, which gives Cardinal Bellarmine the victory over Galileo.

The authors sum up: "A need and craving to be liked, drifting with the crowd, conformity, a kind of passive anti-intellectualism . . . these seem to be the outstanding characteristics of the present-day younger generation." If these children reflect the thinking of their parents, then the old America is finished. I prefer to think that they have drifted into "un-American" ways of thinking through the weakness of our educational system, which can be corrected.

The attitude of the young people is also disturbing in that they are now perfectly vulnerable to any totalitarian-minded group, Left or Right. And those who like to point out that we are a republic, not a democracy, are totalitarian-minded. In their incontinent attacks on those they dislike (anyone favoring any sort of public welfare is a Communist or Comsymp) and by pretending that there is a vast Communist conspiracy inside the United States (it is not inside but outside), they do their best to divide and confuse.

If the Communist pressure upon us were less, I think it unlikely that those radical forces Goldwater is trying to unite would ever take power through the democratic process. The majority is too conservative for that "Conservative." But I can see in a time of national panic the emergence of the first dictatorship in our history. It will come not from the Left but from the Right, and a cynical, indifferent electorate, already contemptuous of the Constitution and the Bill of Rights, will take to it eagerly. When that happens, the American Revolution will be at an end, and lost.

[Associated Press, December 10, 1961.]

THEATER

For a short time near the end of 1959 I was drama critic for the *Reporter*. I wrote a half-dozen pieces and quit because I found attending plays as a duty hard and sometimes embarrassing work. But I did decide early that the only way to review a play usefully was to review not the play as much as the audience's response to what was shown on the stage. I include here four of the pieces for the *Reporter*, as well as a review of Eugene O'Neill's *Touch of the Poet*, written for the *Nation*. These are preceded by a somewhat bravura piece on the commercial theater in our time, called "Love Love Love." It appeared in the *Partisan Review*, and there are still repercussions.

LOVE LOVE LOVE

"Love love love love love love love love love" —
give or take a few "loves" — was the entire lyric of a
song by Charlie Chaplin and I herewith propose that
it be adopted as the American theater's official anthem.
Just name your problem, sit back and let love solve it:
race prejudice, foreign relations — even Job reeling
beneath the unkind attentions of a dubious Yale God
gets off the hook at the end through Love, which has
now replaced the third-act Marines of a simpler time.
On those rare occasions when some other solution tries
to creep into the popular theater it either fails or else
survives only after whatever alien gold was in it has
been transmuted to base Love by the alchemy of production. Granted, Arthur Miller worries his head about
problems of the day; but as for his heart — well,

73

scratched he bleeds Love. Even that attention we must pay his salesman is but a command to love him.

Our popular theater ponders, to the exclusion of all else, the pathos of Love withheld, of Love lost, of Love found after three acts of jittery footling while the man learns Tenderness (never the woman, since, according to commercial lore, Woman *knows*). Moon-guided, triple-crowned, inscrutable, the American Woman in our theater is never so wise as when she's not thinking at all, just being, and listening with a tiny smile to the third-act speech of the man, who has had to learn Tenderness the hard way. "Gosh, Marge, I know how it was, but it won't be like that no more, honest, baby, it won't. No, sir, when I got knocked down in that fight with that two-hundred-pound woman in Salt Lake, I knew what we had was all there is and I'm gonna change, Marge, I swear, because that's all there is, what we got . . . love." And Marge, played by an actress weighing-in at ninety-seven tensely muscular pounds, opens her arms slowly as though semaphoring bad news to a foundering ship; she takes his great, empty buffalo head in her arms. "It's all right, Walter," she says in a voice meant to be tender, though aficionados will detect the approaching kill in this last veronica. "I'm *here,* Walter." And the curtain falls.

Yet in all fairness to our commercial theater, the preoccupation with Love was thrust upon it by the society it reflects or tries to reflect. By Love the theater does not mean love in Rousseau's sense (to employ him as

a Romantic touchstone, pre-Agony). Nor is Love anything quite so simple as successful copulation, though
that of course is of coeval (as Mr. Faulkner would say)
importance. After all, one of the few goals our friendly
society has set us is a more perfect union; the general
failure to achieve it, of course, ensures full employment
to mental therapists, causes dramatic religious conver-
sions and, in the case of one talented theater director,
has driven him to pad obsessively the crotches of the
less flamboyantly hung actors (Aristophanes would
have found a joke in that; we can't). No, Love in our
theater is not really sex though sex is part of it. Love
is a warm druggedness, a surrender of the will and the
mind to inchoate feelings of Togetherness. Thought is
the enemy; any exercise of mind betrays Love, and
Love's vengeance in the theater is terrible, for mind
must be broken and made to recant, and then to love
Love. But before we score the silliness of our popular
theater, we ought to recognize that it reflects, always
more baldly than the novel, say, the superstitions and
prejudices of the age. The flabbiness of tone in the
theater differs only in its oversimplified effects from the
same flabbiness in the popular (and sometimes "serious") novel, and, to get to the root, it does no more
than reflect the ubiquitous flab of the Great Golfer's
reign. Whether Tocqueville's worst fears have come
true or not, democracy is too much with us. It has been
duly noted how often people now say "I feel" such-and-
such to be true rather than "I think" such-and-such to

be true. To make that shift of verb unconsciously is to eschew mind and take cover in the cozier, more democratic world of feeling. I suppose there are some who say of others pejoratively, "His feelings are not deep." But if pressed, they would admit that no one really knows what another's feelings are, though it is of course agreed that we are all pretty much alike at heart: sensitive, warm, tender, our moments of bad behavior the result of the green twig's early bending, sure to straighten and flower beneath Love's therapeutic sun. In any case, in our theater feeling is all, and the deliberate exercise of mind is thought an admission of emotional poverty. Particularly mistrusted is Bernard Shaw, whose works are dismissed as displays of debater's tricks, the plots suitable only for adaptation to musical comedy. He did not love Love; worse, he made the devil a Love-lover, and chose as hero Don Juan, a mere life-lover.

Now it is almost too easy to put down Broadway. So much of what's wrong is so obvious that most attacks on our theater lose force because of the target's size. It is impossible with a shotgun at three paces not to hit the Shubert Theater. Yet it is curious how often the serious-minded do miss the essential target. For instance, not long ago a lively young critic fired a familiar blast: no ideas in our theater, too many sensational productions *épater le box office,* too many writers revealing sexual obsessions of depressing singularity. All the usual changes were rung, but then the critic entitled his piece "The Theater Is Losing Its Minds," and confused everything. I don't know how far back his memory, both actual and learned, goes, but if there were ever any minds operative in the American theater it is news to me. Before Eugene O'Neill (whose mastery of ideas was second to none, unless it be his fellow Nobelist Pearl Buck), there was a wasteland of Owen Davises, Avery Hopwoods and Eugene Walters, stretching back to the egregious Royall Tyler, who started the American theater on its mindless way. Two centuries of junk. If anything, there are rather more signs of intelligence stirring now than in the bad old days.

A few months later, our critic was back again. This time he wondered why the better novelists did not bring "mind" to the theater. Or at least why hadn't the theater produced playwrights as good as the novelists on today's List, and he gave the List, betraying himself, I'm afraid, as an incipient Love-lover. Parenthetically, each year there is a short List of the O.K. Writers. Today's List consists of two Jews, two Negroes and a safe floating *goy* of the old American Establishment (often Wright Morris), just to show there is no prejudice in our Loving world; only the poor old homosexuals are out. It is a list dictated not by any aesthetic but by Good Citizenship. That the writers on it happen to be admirable is irrelevant: Togetherness put them there and we all feel better seeing them belaureled. My young critic is not responsible for today's List, but he showed a certain absence of mind in trying to beat the playwrights with it, because not one of the writers named could be thought of as an intellectual in the sense I assumed he meant (Gide, Camus, even the dervish Genet). They are all good, if fairly standard, writers, more or less in the naturalistic tradition, and, at least in their novels, betray no more mind than do the plays of Arthur Miller.

I find this sort of mistake (taking good writers of one sort and saying they are good writers of quite another sort on the grounds that to be good is good enough) yet another sign of the general corruption of aesthetic and intellectual values in this soft age. The language of criticism now tends to be as inexact as the prose of the works criticized. No one seems to know who or what anyone or anything is. Prevalent is a lazy permissiveness. Our literature as well as our theater seems at times like a terrible kindergarten. Jack is a great novelist because he *feels* he's a great novelist. Anything goes. I am sometimes charmed by the minor talent of J. D. Salinger, but when he puts on his Great Author suit I think one should point out that it doesn't fit. On every side counterfeit talents flood the exchange. This was always so, but in other times and places there were certain critics whose bite authenticated coinage. They are still with us — but outside the battle, in the Academy.

I have often thought it would be a service to the audience if each writer was forced to refer to himself in a certain style and manner which would make clear what he is. Implicitly, each does, but it is confusing to all but a student of rhetoric. Arthur Miller (he is on my mind because I have just read the Preface to his collected plays) writes of himself not seriously but solemnly. With paralyzing pomp, splitting his infinitives and confusing number, he climbs the steps to the throne, with the enemy syntax crushed beneath his heavy boot: he is our prophet, our king, our guide in the dark. The only thing wrong is that he does not write awfully well. In other times, if one had made such a criticism it would have been quite enough. But Mr. Miller is ready for this stricture (and so are all the other hackers in the kindergarten). "We have had," he reminds those of us who were nodding, "more than one extraordinary dramatist who was a cripple as a writer, and this is lamentable but not ruinous." I suppose he could get out of that one by saying he meant extraordinary to mean just that: extra-ordinary, though of course there is nothing more ordinary than writer-cripples in our theater.

Now by needling the pretensions of Mr. Miller (whom I often admire as a writer-cripple), I don't mean to scout his rightful position in the commercial theater — he is more good than bad as an influence and as a fact — but to draw attention again to the lack of any sense in our aesthetic judgments. Mr. Miller — and all the rest — can get away with just about any evaluation he wants to make of himself, and those who know differently won't bother to straighten out the matter for an audience which seems perfectly content to receive counterfeit bills for checks drawn in good faith. What we need are fewer ontological critics (*pace* John Crowe Ransom) and more critics like Mary McCarthy, who will remind the kindergarteners that though they can have as much fun as they want, at some point the line between fantasy and reality must be firmly drawn. No, you are *not* a poet; you are you. As it is now, even our abler commentators are so many Madame Verdurins, eager, shrewd but confused as to true precedence. And the noncounterfeit artist must either go in to table last or make a fool of himself, much as the Baron de Charlus did that curious afternoon.

I happen to like a number of playwrights as people. For some reason they bring out my protective and pedagogic instincts. I like to reassure them, to help them, to give them reading lists. In many ways they are to be admired for stamina, since to be produced on Broadway resembles nothing so much as being shot from a cannon at a fragile net. One should not be surprised if the more sensitive dramatists tend to get a bit punchy. Most of them (I am generalizing hugely, but life is short) experience serious difficulty in reading books, which necessarily limits their fund of general information on any subject not connected with the theater or their own psychoanalysis. The literary world, to the extent they are aware of it at all, seems to them an invidious establishment where writers dislike them because they are better known and make more money than any other sort of writer. They do not realize that, having no interest in language and even less in what we like to think of as mind, they necessarily must earn the contempt of those who do bother with such things. The result is that although in its essential preoccupations our theater cannot help but reflect the day, it has always been estranged not only from its own country's culture but, to strike that minatory gong, from Western civilization. The result has been a curiously artificial development, resembling nothing but itself, like those amoebae which when boxed upon a slide stop their anarchic zooming about and make perfect right angles, as tribute to an imposed environment.

"Weariness of the theatre is the prevailing note of London criticism. Only the ablest critics believe that the theatre is really important; in my time, none of them would claim for it, as I claimed for it, that it is as important as the Church was in the Middle Ages. . . ." Ah, that crisp hopeful voice! Shaw in 1906. "A theatre to me is a place where two or three are 'gathered together.' The apostolic succession from Eschylus to myself is as serious and as continuously inspired as that younger institution, the apostolic succession of the Christian Church." Brave words and perhaps true, though there have not been very many American gatherings-together one would like William Morris to attend. With some justice, intellectuals hold our popular theater in contempt, and one of the reasons seldom explicitly stated is not so much the meretriciousness of the exhibits — popular art is opportunist at best — as its moments of would-be seriousness. Milton Berle telling low-comedy jokes onstage can be very beguiling; but to be lectured to in a stern tone by a writer considerably more stupid than much of his audience is a somber experience, and were our collective manners not better, theater seats would be torn up and hurled at the stage. Earnest Neanderthals implore us not to persecute minority groups; they exhort us to tenderness; they inform us that war is destructive; they remind us that love is the only connection. There is nothing wrong with these themes except the blunt obviousness with which they are handled and the self-righteous tone of writers whose aesthetic derives partly from mental therapists and partly from those urgent dramas that once made radio wonderful. It is not that one does not admire Arthur Miller's real gifts for theater-writing or his good heart. It is his stunning solemnity which annoys. Stop telling us what we already know! And don't write sentences like: "That he had not the intellectual fluency to verbalize his situation is not the same thing as saying that he lacked awareness, even an overly intensified consciousness that the life he had made was without form and inner meaning." That is not a writer writing or a man trying to get through to others; it is the voice of the holder of a degree in Education. One sympathizes with Mr. Miller's passion to be admired, to be thought significant. All of us tend more or less consciously to arrange our personas in an attractive way. But his attempt is saddening because, though he is not taken seriously outside the popular theater and press, he is *almost* good enough to be respected in the way he wants. More to the point, he *should* be good enough: I attribute his failure to the popular theater's estrangement from the country's culture.

In the last fifteen years the French theater has been used by Gide, Sartre, Camus, de Montherlant, Genet, Anouilh, Julian Green, Giraudoux — an eclectic list which goes on and on, comprising most of the better French writers. And what have we had? Tennessee Williams (whom I happen to admire), Mr. Miller, one small mood play by Carson McCullers, Thornton Wilder in his later, three-cheers-for-Love manner, and, of course, the heady splendors of *J.B.* It is not a heartening record.

The cult of feeling has not only undone much of our theater writing, it has also peculiarly victimized those gentle souls, the actors. They have been taught that "truth" is everything. And what is "truth"? Feeling. And what is feeling? Their own secret core, to which the character they are to interpret must be related. To listen to actors talk about "truth" is a chilling experience. They employ a kind of solemn baby talk compounded of analysts' jargon and the arcane prose of the late Stanislavsky. As one of them said severely of another's performance: "He's not thinking; he's only thinking he's thinking." Our actors have also been taught to condemn the better English or French actors as "technical."

"Technical" here *seems* to mean — in these circles words are employed for transient emotive effects, never meaning — that a separation has been made between the actor's own feelings and those the part he is playing calls for. To understand just who Iago is, the "technical" actor will deliberately make the separation. Then, having got the proper range, he will, by an effort of will, inhabit the character, using himself as much or as little as he pleases, his goal being the interpretation of Shakespeare's Iago, *not* the revelation of his own inner state as he grapples with Iago. Our actors may not be able to say a line of verse intelligibly or begin to understand what Iago is all about, but you can bet they will bring floods of irrelevant feelings to the part. It is not acting but group therapy. And the sad thing is that though this kind of acting is usually disagreeable to watch, it is delightful to do. They won't change without a struggle; and since they feel rather than think, they tend to be fanatics about a method whose queen, of course, is the genuinely gifted Kim Stanley. Yet the whole sad mistaken thing is all there in her large bland face, the small eyes turned inward though they seem to be looking out, the whiny voice rising and falling according to the beat of some inner metronome of "truth," her whole being suffused in a nimbus of self-love. The final effect is onanistic.

For some years I would not read Mary McCarthy's theater criticism, after her majestically wrongheaded estimate of *A Streetcar Named Desire*. She not only missed the point to the play but, worse, got carried away by irrelevancies: Williams was really a slob, devoted to success, pretending to be a real artist while swinging with the Broadway set; worst of all, he was guilty of "ambition." She uses this word several times in her collected pieces to tick off those writers who try, sneakily, to get above their talents. Art climbers are very like social climbers, and Miss McCarthy is a good one to put each in his place. Now I grant that there is something odd in Tennessee Williams's work which not only enrages otherwise reasonable critics but drives them to impute motives to him which are more the business of post-mortem biography than of criticism. I think again of the young critic who wrote recently in *Encounter* that Williams's real theme was incest. Well, his real theme is *not* incest no matter how one chooses to read the plays. One does not dare speculate on what sort of grapevine gossip led to this conclusion; thought certainly had nothing to do with it, though feeling might. But aside from Miss McCarthy's forty whacks at Williams, when I finally came to read her collected criticism I was struck by her remarkable good sense. She is certainly the best American writer to have written about the American theater in our generation. Uncorrupted by compassion, her rather governessy severity, even cruelty, derives from the useful knowledge that the road to kitsch is paved with good ambitions, and that one must not give the "A" for ambition without also giving simultaneously the "E" for the poor thing effected. The theater needs continual reminders that there is nothing more debasing than the work of those who do well what is not worth doing at all.

A minor phenomenon of the theater today is the milieu: kitchens in Kansas, cold-water flats, Bronx apartments, the lower-middle-class venue depicted in naturalistic terms by "truthful" actors before an audience of overdressed, overfed burghers. How does that audience stand it, even when it's good? Is it that they enjoy a nostalgic *frisson* at looking back to their own origins? Or is there a desire to know about things today, to be instructed by the narcissism of a John Osborne, who tells them: "This is the way we are, young, angry, unique"? The burghers nod and belch softly, and some doze: it is the theater of the editorial and the survey. Even those who dislike Tennessee Williams must give him credit for castrating a hero here, eating one there; and with Elia Kazan racketing the actors about the stage, it is not easy to sleep. I save any further defense of Williams for another occasion, since my intention in these notes is entirely destructive.

And where do we go from here? I confess I have no very clear notion of what I should like to see the theater become. As a playwright I am a sport, whose only serious interest is the subversion of a society that bores and appalls me (no world elsewhere, alas; this is the one to fix). Yet I don't see much change for the good. Plays cost too much to put on. That means investors will be wary of new things. I also suspect that despite the enviable example of the French, our comparable good writers are not apt to be much of an improvement on the ones already in the theater. In England, the Royal Court Theatre has offered hospitality to some of the better writers, but the plays so far produced have been disappointing. In fact, it may very well be that the simplemindedness we score in our playwrights is a necessary characteristic of play-making.

In any case, there is no use in worrying about Broadway. Expect less rather than more intelligence on the stage, especially as costs increase. Revel in the graver efforts, which will more and more resemble *J.B.* — that portentous magnum of chloroform Elia Kazan so accurately broke across our collective brows, launching us upon a glum sea anodyne. In fact, the former Assistant Secretary of State may well have got our Age's number back in the 1930's, when he decided that a poem should not mean but be. Our theater certainly does not mean; it is. Yet to the extent that it is, it mirrors us. Look in it and you will see quite plain the un-Loved face of Caliban.

[*Partisan Review,* Spring 1959.]

EUGENE O'NEILL'S "A TOUCH OF THE POET"

Seven or perhaps eleven plays to encompass all things American from the Revolution to The Way We Live Now. Then after a number of false starts, the solemn burning of aborted fragments in a hotel room in Boston with only one completed play surviving, *A Touch of the Poet*, set in 1828. What could sound more unpromising? Especially in the wake of the self-indulgent *Long Day's Journey into Night*, whose production and reception on Broadway resembled nothing so much as a state funeral, with black plumes waving and sonorous eulogies of the dead master from those who gave so little aid and comfort to the living master for his *The Iceman Cometh* in 1946.

I went to the theater expecting the worst. Even before the curtain went up, irritable phrases formed in my mind (how often, I wonder, does this happen to professional reviewers?). "Rhetoric is the attempt of the will to do the work of the imagination" — W. B. Yeats. . . . I would definitely use that one, for if there was ever a rhetorician it was O'Neill. Then I recalled my old resentment against his misuse of the *Oresteia* when, having crudely borrowed the relationships, the melodrama, the tension of Aeschylus, he blithely left out the whole idea of justice, which was the point to that trilogy. And, finally, the maddening urge of American primitives to include everything — to write cycles, tetralogies, epics — the whole hee-haw of the Thomas Wolfes as they list the rivers of America in alphabetical order, their minds innocent of civilization, their self-love filling the empty plains of a new continent which *ought* to have a tragedy, though just what it is no one has yet discovered.

The curtain rose. Two minor characters started talking. My heart sank as they explained at length necessary secrets. Then suddenly the stage was bathed in light. Helen Hayes and Kim Stanley were on; the drama had begun and O'Neill blazed.

A Touch of the Poet is a beautiful play, beautifully presented. It has but one fault (to which I shall come last), for which its virtues more than compensate. The play is *rose*, not *noire*, and it has a deliberate artifice that I prefer to the shapeless black melodramas O'Neill latterly preferred. Then, too, 1828 is just right: Andrew Jackson; the rise of the Democrats; the fall of J. Q.

Adams and with him that oligarchical, gentlemanly society which began the nation. All this is symbolically right, and pleasing. It is time we used our bit of history, especially since the New York audience has no real sense of the United States before the First World War. Lincoln, of course, is recalled glumly; it is known that there was some sort of revolution at the beginning; and that's it — almost as if Van Wyck Brooks had never lived.

O'Neill reminds us of our past. He indicates the rise of the Yankee merchants — busy, practical, contemptuous of the old aristocratic principle. With precision and uncharacteristic economy, O'Neill sets the scene for his moral action, which is the crushing of a man's false pride, his absorption into the main, his final realization that he has lived a bogus life, presuming to a position both worldly and moral to which he has no right but the one — and this is significant — of wanting.

Cornelius Melody (Eric Portman) was born of Irish peasants, served bravely in the Peninsular campaign, became a British officer, got a peasant girl pregnant, married her, came to America, opened a tavern and failed. He torments his wife (Helen Hayes) and his daughter (Kim Stanley). He quotes Byron to himself in a mirror. He assumes the manner of a king in exile. He is laughed at by the Yankees but adored by his wife, who understands him perhaps more profoundly in O'Neill-land than she would in life. She sees how lonely he is in his vanity (very Meredithian, this), and she loves him. He is alternately mocked and served by his daughter, a finely realized character; part dreamer, part materialist, veering this way and that, ambivalent and strange.

The story is simple. The daughter loves a Yankee of the new merchant class. He has escaped his family to write poetry but eventually he will go into business — happily. The girl must marry him to escape the world of unpaid bills and false pride. She also loves him and wants to cheat neither of them. His family deplores the match. They try to buy her off. Dressed in his British army uniform, Melody, drunk, goes to challenge the boy's father to a duel; he is beaten up by the police; he returns, pride gone, and in an incredible *volte-face* chooses reality to prideful illusion: he is only a Mick and a failure who loves his wife. The girl gets her Yankee, and all ends well.

What makes the play work thematically is the examination of Melody's dream world. It may well be that this is the most significant American theme of the twentieth century. Since reality did not please him, he chose to invent his own past. He told lies; he believed the lies and for various reasons was abetted in his fantasies by those about him. O'Neill has often dealt with this theme (*The Iceman Cometh*, for example) and so have many of our best writers, most notably Tennessee Williams in *A Streetcar Named Desire*.

Which brings us to an interesting question: What is it in modern American life (1828 is as good a date as any to start the "modern") which forces so many to prefer fantasy to reality? One observes the fantastifiers at every cocktail party: charming people, boring people, intelligent, dull — people of all sorts, telling lies, which no one much minds. It is all a game. Who shall I be? Who am I? And the person who drops the brick of truth is the only villain.

It is to this that the audience of *A Touch of the Poet* most responds. There is an element of Melody in all of us, and one watches with horrified fascination as he is brought at last to the truth about himself.

The production is good. Harold Clurman has taken the three most mannered actresses in our theater and imposed the play's manner on them with complete success. Miss Hayes is strong and direct and very moving, her usual cute pony-prancing severely curbed. Betty Field, whose old voice I always liked, has a new one which works admirably in her single scene. But the production's glory is Kim Stanley's performance. The old annoying tricks are still there, but now they glitter and she gets the character's ambivalence with such fairness that one is reminded of a character in Dostoevsky: light and shadow mysteriously fluctuating; the "yes" and the simultaneous "no." It is fine work.

The production's only flaw is the performance of Eric Portman. He is a fine technical actor whose attack here is unfortunately wrong. He belongs to what I call the "voice-music" school of English acting, whose honorary president is Sir Ralph Richardson. The voice-musicians hear some strange melody in the wings to which in counterpoint they sing their lines. Their songs are often fascinating but almost always irrelevant to the play's meaning. Mr. Portman is far better in the small neat plays of Terence Rattigan, because in the naturalistic idiom one can gobble and honk and sigh and mumble and the meaning will remain clear. Major Melody needs grandeur and thought, neither of which Mr. Portman provides. As I watched him strut about the stage on his spindly legs, his swollen body held tightly erect, like a pineapple on two sticks, I was haunted by *déjà vu*. Not until the final scene did I recall whom he reminded me of: a maleficent Mr. Micawber — and the moment one plays Melody like Micawber, O'Neill is brought down.

Happily, there are so many good things in this production — including the play — that the thing works, and one is pleased that Eugene O'Neill's final statement should be at once so human and so gently wise.

[The *Nation*, October 25, 1958.]

BERNARD SHAW'S
"HEARTBREAK HOUSE"

"HEARTBREAK HOUSE . . . rhapsodized about love; but it believed in cruelty. It was afraid of the cruel people; and it saw that cruelty was at least effective. Cruelty did things that made money, whereas Love did nothing but prove the soundness of La Rochefoucauld's saying that very few people would fall in love if they had never read about it. Heartbreak House in short did not know how to live, at which point all that was left to it was the boast that at least it knew how to die: a melancholy accomplishment which the outbreak of war presently gave it practically unlimited opportunities of displaying. Thus were the first-born of Heartbreak House smitten; and the young, the innocent, the hopeful expiated the folly and worthlessness of their elders."

That is from Bernard Shaw's odd preface to his even

94

odder play, now revived at the Billy Rose Theater. The preface is odd, among other things, because it is written with the wrong sort of hindsight. Shaw did not know when he began the play in 1913 that the first-born were going to be struck down. Nor is there any reference to war, actual or impending, in the first two acts. The third act, however, was completed after the first aerial bombardments in history, and Shaw, rather casually, uses this to drop a bomb and end the play. Yet it is not the residents of Heartbreak House or their first-born who get blown up; only a businessman and a burglar expiate the folly and worthlessness of . . . what? Not Heartbreak House certainly; capitalism, perhaps.

Everything about the play is queer, even its production history. Plans to put it on during the war went awry. Shaw finally published it, with preface, in 1919. Not until 1920 was the play produced, in New York. The next year it got to the West End. The preface is unique in Shaw for its bitterness and hysteria, and the play . . . well, there are those who put it first among his work and there are those who don't know what to think of it. I'm afraid after seeing it performed for the first time the other day that I liked it a good deal less than I thought I did from having read it; parenthetically, I should put quite plainly here at the beginning that I regard Bernard Shaw as the best and most useful dramatist in English since the author of *Much Ado About Nothing* turned gentleman and let fall the feather.

What is Heartbreak House? In the context of the play it stands for the ruling class of England pre-1914: the "nice people," somewhat educated, somewhat sensitive, somewhat independent financially (their cousins the hearties lived over at Horseback Hall). They were devotees of laissez-faire; they rhapsodized about love — but I have already quoted Shaw's indictment. Heartbreak House, of course, is only another name for our new friend the Establishment, a protective association made up of public-school boys who come down from Oxbridge to take over Whitehall, the Church of England, the BBC, Fleet Street, the better-looking girls, and everything else that's fun, while (so young writers tell us) sneering at the newly articulate *Lumpenproletariat* who have gone to red-brick colleges where, if one reads the new novels accurately, the main course given is Opportunism: Don't reform, adapt. The jocose nihilism of many of the anti-Establishment novels and plays is no more than a love-hate acceptance of the Establishment; the Kingsley Amises approach it on its own terms in a way Shaw would have detested. Where he would have leveled Heartbreak House to make way for a carefully planned housing project, the new attackers of the Establishment merely want to move into some of those nice rooms at the top, an attitude ignoble to a socialist and hopelessly petty to an outsider who is aware that the rooms at the top of a diminished England are not much better than those directly under. The Establishment has only an island to tend, while

Heartbreak House, with Asquith and Bonar Law and Ramsay Mac for weekend guests, governed much of the world. To put it plain, Shaw's target was important; and he knew what he wanted, which was not to adapt, or to make his own way, but to reform.

I think we know pretty much what Shaw intended to do in *Heartbreak House,* yet what actually did he do in the play itself? For one thing, it is improvised work. Shaw admitted he made it up as he went along, not knowing from day to day what his characters would do or say or become. He always tended to work this way, regarding a play essentially as an organism with a life of its own; one need only nurture it and let it assume its own shape. He even used to keep a kind of checkerboard at hand to remind him who was onstage and who was off at any given moment in the writing. There is no doubt this method served him as well as any other; his night mind was not, to say the least, fantastic. I am sure deep in his unconscious there lurked not the usual nightmare monsters of the rest of us but yards of thesis, antithesis, and synthesis, all neatly labeled and filed. Yet in *Heartbreak House* Shaw's improvisatory genius breaks down; he keeps marching into conversational culs-de-sac.

For example, in the second act the play comes to a grinding halt after Boss Mangan, recovered from hypnotic trance, denounces and is denounced by those who happen to be onstage at the moment, and exits. Then Captain Shotover tosses a Delphic phrase or two upon the night and paddles off. (Later the Captain, while again trying for an exit, says, almost apologetically: "I must go in and out," a compulsion he shares with everyone else in this play; they all go in and out at whim.) This ill-madeness is often beguiling except on those occasions when it defeats the author, who finds himself with nobody left onstage except a couple who don't have much of anything to say to one another at the moment. It is then that Shaw invariably, shamelessly, brings on the New Character, who is very often a member of the lower classes with a colorful speech pattern usually written out phonetically in the text. This time he is the Burglar, a comic character right out of Dickens, where Shaw claimed, not entirely facetiously, to have got most of his characters, at least those who are not himself. The Burglar is one of Shaw's standbys, used in play after play; he is awful, but at least he starts the second act moving again and gives it a certain vivacity. As usual, Shaw, delighted with his own cunning, starts tying up ends; the Burglar is really the Captain's old bos'n, the nurse's husband, etc., etc. And now let's have a long chat about the poor and the exploited, the exploiters and the *rentiers,* and then end the act.

As a rule, Shaw's arbitrariness does not disturb. After all, he is conducting a seminar with enormous wit and style and we don't much mind his more casual contrivances. But in this play they don't come off. I think it has to do with a fundamental conflict between characters and settings. The characters, of course, are our old friends the Bernard Shaw Team of Fabian Debaters; we know each one of them already. But what are they doing in this peculiar Midsummer's Eve *ambiance?* They seem a bit puzzled, too. As they debate with their usual ease they tend nervously to eye the shrubbery: are there elves at the bottom of that garden? Have we been booked into an allegory? Are we going to find out we're all dead or something? Steady, chaps, the old boy's got us into one of *those* plays. They rattle on bravely but they are clearly ill at ease, and so is the audience. I think it was one of the New York daily critics who observed that the mood is not Chekhov but J. M. Barrie. Which is exactly right. We are led to expect magic, fey girls upon the heath, and revelation through fantasy. But we get none of it. Instead we are offered the old Debating Team in top form but in the wrong place and mood (oh, for that dentist's office!). As a result the debaters recede as characters; we grow indifferent to them; they are too humorous in the original sense of the word. Especially Ellie, Shaw's supergirl. In this version she is more than ever iron, ready to mother not heroes but heroines. Shaw dotes on Ellie; I found her purest drip-torture. Halfway through the play I had a startling *aperçu:* Shaw regarded himself not as a man or an artist or a social meliorist but as a kind of superwoman, a chaste spinster fiercely armed with the umbrella of dialectic, asexual limbs bluestockinged, and tongue wagging. Of all the debaters assembled, I liked only Captain Shotover, because his dottiness contrasted agreeably with the uneasy predictability of his teammates.

Finally, at the play's end, I found myself entirely confused as to what Shaw intended. Shaw is not, even when he would like to be, an impressionist, a Chekhov turning life before our eyes to no end but that life observed is sufficient. *Look, we live, we are,* says Chekhov. While Shaw declares briskly: *Pull up your socks! Fall in line there. Come along now. Double-quick march and we'll overtake the future by morning!* One loves Shaw for his optimism, but moonlight is not a time for marching, and *Heartbreak House* is a moonlight play, suitable for recapturing the past; but moonlight is a hopeless time for making plans. Elegy and debate cancel one another out. Nor is the work really satiric, an attack on "folly and worthlessness." These people are splendid and unique, and Shaw knows it. He had no intention of blowing them up at the end.

Shaw's prefaces — no matter how proudly irrelevant their content may, at first, seem to the play that follows (sometimes a bit forlornly) — usually turn out to be apposite or at least complementary. But not this preface. In fact, it is misleading. Shaw talks about Chekhov. He finds the country-house mentality Chekhov *seems* to be writing about endemic to Europe, part of the sweet sickness of the bourgeoisie. Therefore Shaw will examine the same house in the same way, only in English terms. Ever since that preface, we have all dutifully considered this play in terms of Chekhov. Does it compare? Is it as good? Why is it *unlike?* Brooks Atkinson recently remarked that Chekhov's dying fall does not suit Shaw, who never dies and never falls, who stands ready with a program for every need. This is certainly true, yet I have a hunch that if Shaw had not given us a false lead, none of us would have ever thought of comparing him to Chekhov. True, both are dealing with the same dying society of "nice people," but where Chekhov's interest was the "nice people," Shaw's interest was the dying society and the birth pains of the new.

Shaw once told Sir Cedric Hardwicke that he had no idea how to end the play until the first bombs fell. I suspect he had originally planned to allow Captain Shotover to attain "the Seventh Degree of concentration," thereby detonating the dynamite he had stored in the gravel pit and blowing up the enemy Mangan. As it was, at the last minute, the bomb from the Zeppelin did the trick even better, providing Shaw quite literally with a god from the machine. Then, almost as an afterthought, Shaw comes to the point:

HECTOR: Well, I don't mean to be drowned like a rat in a trap. I still have the will to live. What am I to do?

CAPTAIN SHOTOVER: Do? Nothing simpler. Learn your business as an Englishman.

HECTOR: And what may my business as an Englishman be, pray?

CAPTAIN SHOTOVER: Navigation. Learn it and live; or leave it and be damned.

And that's it. Captain Shotover, supposed to have sold his soul to the devil, to have meddled with mysticism, to have mastered the *non sequitur*, turns out to be a good Fabian socialist after all. Obviously, Shotover was a humbug mystic, excusably deranged by the setting Shaw put him in; not until faced with his world's extinction does he throw off the mask of dottiness to reveal the bright, hard, intelligent face of Bernard Shaw, who to this day has a good deal to tell us about the danger of a society drifting as opposed to one which has learned the virtue of setting a deliberate course by fixed stars. To navigate is to plan. Laissez-faire, though always delightful for a few, in crisis is disastrous for all. There is no alternative to a planned society; that is the burden of the Shaw debate. Almost as an afterthought he makes this familiar point as the bomb drops near Heartbreak House.

The production now on view is ambitious, and at many points successful. As usual, I found myself more attentive to the audience than to the play. As they say in physics, there is no action without reaction. I can think of no urgent reason for writing about productions in the theater unless one also writes about the audience, too. The play acts upon the audience, which is society today; the audience reacts and in its reaction one can get a sense of the superstitions and prejudices which obtain. Theater can be revelatory. In fact, I wish sociologists would spend more time in the theater and less in conducting polls and drawing graphs. Any audience at *Tea and Sympathy* or *Auntie Mame* will tell them more about the way we live now than a house-to-house canvass from Morristown to White Plains with pad and pencil.

In the case of an old play like *Heartbreak House* one may also use it as a touchstone. In the 1920's it seemed one thing, in the 1930's another, and so on. To those watching, the day I saw it, *Heartbreak House* was a delightful place, menaced by burglars, self-made men, and Zeppelins. The clothes were chic yet quaint and every woman saw herself up there pouring tea for weak enamored men who tended to burst into tears while the ladies talked a bright blue streak. Whenever the debate really got going, 1959's attention flagged: Is that a rubber plant? Can they still get egret feathers or is that an imitation? Did you leave the keys in the car? . . . Bernard Shaw, I'm afraid, was being taken for Oscar Wilde, and afflicted with un-Wildean *longueurs*. To put it bluntly, we are not used to debate at any level. If Bernard Shaw, who made the act of argument as pleasurable as any writer who ever lived, cannot hold his audience except by predictable paradoxes and references to adultery and all the familiar junk of the Commercialites, we the audience are in a bad way. Although in fairness it must be admitted that talking about society and the better life and planning of any sort has never been a characteristic of the Anglo-American mind.

Nevertheless, Harold Clurman had directed this production just as though we were really awake out there and knew what was going on. He is enormously helped by Diana Wynyard and Pamela Brown, who are beautifully right for this kind of thing. Maurice Evans, an actor I seem to like only as Richard II no matter what else he plays, is unexpectedly fine as Captain Shotover. I'm not sure dressing up to look like Bernard Shaw was a wise idea; I suspect Shaw would have hated it; but it does help Mr. Evans to hide beneath whiskers and putty the self-pitying face of Richard II, and I could not have liked him more. Sam Levene of course was all wrong as Boss Mangan. He is a good *farceur*, but in another style, and his scenes tended to throw everyone else off: it was not unlike casting our own beloved Marjorie Main as Lady Bracknell. The other weak link is Diane Cilento as Ellie, the supergirl. Miss Cilento plays with a grinding monotony made worse because she has gone and got herself one of those Voices. Let me explain. Right after the war, Pamela Brown's most lovely strange diction was the ambition and despair of every English girl on the stage. We got Miss Brown's Voice in every possible key. Then there was heard in the land Joan Greenwood's hoarse, intimate rasp, to our delight and her peers' despair. Now Miss Cilento has distilled herself a voice which is two-parts Brown and one-part Greenwood, and I think she ought to give it up, right now. She is a beautiful girl with some talent; yet if Ellie is to be made less than revolting she must be played with as little artifice and as much "naturalness" as possible. I daresay Mr. Clurman was aware of this, but sooner get a bird to sing Mozart than force an actress to discard a Voice she has worked on. All in all, reservations about this particular play aside, I hope it runs forever and gives heart to those who expect the theater to be something more than a business for those who, in their calculated desire to please us, only make us more than ever absent of mind.

[The *Reporter*, November 26, 1959.]

THE COMMERCIALITES

T<small>HE DESIRE</small> to give pleasure is a fundamental characteristic of the popular artist, nor is it necessarily a meretricious one: Shakespeare was an instinctive pleasure giver, and in our own time Tennessee Williams possesses in abundance (I nearly wrote "suffers from") this particular trait. The literary pleasure givers are happiest using the theater, loneliest in the novel. Even Charles Dickens, an archetypal pleasure giver, turned finally to the stage as performer. And it is understandable. A most tangible audience responds like a lover to pleasure given, and in his audience's response the artist is himself ravished by what he has done. The result is a beautiful circle of love which at its truest has been responsible for much good art in the theater along with most of the bad.

Opposed to the pleasure givers are the polemicist,

the satirist, the nauseated, the reformer. In short, those writers whose primary objective is the criticism of a society which is in essential conflict with the writer's own sense of what life should be. Bernard Shaw is paradigmatic. His pleasure giving was deliberately calculated to disguise polemic intent as sugar does harsh medicine. (This was his own metaphor; to which a friend answered: "How clever of the public to lick off the sugar and leave your pill undigested!")

Americans of the mid-century, eager to be loved, have produced very few writers in the theater of this second kind — perhaps the odd George Kelly; Arthur Miller at moments . . . and the list trails off. Even an "intellectual" like Thornton Wilder is, finally, as pleasure-giving and mind-withholding as all the other cocker spaniels who prance about Times Square, tails wagging, eyes glowing with love — simulated or real: it makes no difference as they go about demanding love for pleasure given.

Ultimately, of course, what matters is the work, not the motives of those who made it. But I suggest that when the work accomplished exploits too crudely our prejudices and weaknesses, it is difficult not to ask: "*Why* are they doing this to us? For what end?" Now to be commercial in the theater is, simply, to try to make money out of a basic investment of time, money and talent. There is no other kind of theater in America, nor will there be as long as plays cost as much as they do to mount. If we had a Bernard Shaw among us, and if he thought it might be useful (and to him, if not to us, pleasurable) to write a play showing that democracy is a disaster, or that Christianity is a bitter hoax, he would not be produced. That in itself is not necessarily the end of the matter. He could still use the novel, the essay, the published play, which could make its effect slowly upon readers and find peripheral production. But the working dramatist must either not do what interests him the most, or disguise it entirely, or — and here is the real tragedy of commercialism — discard automatically any idea or theme which he knows is not acceptable to the prejudices of an audience that must be won by flattery and charm. No American dramatist in the last war would have written with such virulence against President Roosevelt as Aristophanes wrote against the Athenian Establishment at a time of war and national disaster. Yet our dramatists cannot be scored for not attempting the impossible. Large societies are difficult to assault. Novelists are let alone, for they have little public effect. The *Nation* may attack J. Edgar Hoover until the hoods come home, and the watchman will still cry "All's well!" But to use the theater or television for stating ideas that do not give immediate pleasure to a large bland audience is to experience harsh censorship; it is either not done at all or else so distorted in the doing that the result is neither one thing nor the other.

The Crucible, by Arthur Miller, was much attacked when it was first produced during the great days of the

Wisconsin buffoon. Yet there is nothing in this good if rather glum little play which breaks new ground, which demonstrates anything but an old saw or two about bearing false witness and the panicky response of a weak-minded society to psychotics. I should think a playwright really daring if he were to show us dramatically that Communism or socialism or fascism is superior to democratic *laissez faire*. One might disagree, but at least we should have a new theme to consider. But this may not happen, for the inner censor is at work. To me that is the most terrible result of commercialism.

I remember how in the so-called Golden Age of television, writers were continually (and rightfully) chafing under network and advertising-agency censorship. To a man they wanted freedom. But when asked "Freedom to do what?" they would become evasive and tentative. Well, to be able to use four-letter words and naturalistic expletives the way the novelists do; to defend minority groups openly; to be allowed to call a Jew a Jew and not the weirdly generalized "He's one of *them*" (knowing wink) "and we know what *they* are!" — this much latitude would certainly be welcome, but it is not much to dream of. American popular writers (like their Russian counterparts) are prisoners of the state, sentenced for life. They want yard privileges and better food, but they shrink at the idea of choice, of life outside the familiar walls of superstition that we call the free world. I suspect, barring accident, that the next generation will prove both to the Soviet and to us how much alike great states are in the twentieth century, and how undesirable to those states true freedom is. The most dangerous and successful censorship is inner censorship. In this our Commercialites are anticipating the future.

Among the Commercialites, the team of Jerome Lawrence and Robert E. Lee is typical. I did not see their admired *Inherit the Wind,* but I did see something of theirs called *Auntie Mame.* Now they have run up a play about the Harding Administration. One wonders why. They have nothing to say about the political process in America, nothing to say about Harding and his associates. Sensing that they had no theme, they announced to the press shortly before the opening that their urgent message to the nation was "Beware government by crony!" But that is not an issue. Nowadays not even the vilest Presidential crony could steal as blithely as those in the play do. There are too many checks. Like the rest of our citizenry, politicians are congenitally inclined to dishonesty, but these days the dishonesty is intellectual and moral, not financial. In the glare of publicity at a national level there is little opportunity to steal anything except power.

Only one interesting thing happened in the theater the night I saw *The Gang's All Here.* When the Attorney General delivered an impassioned speech about the virtue of getting ahead and the obligation each individual has to himself to get all he can by any means, honest or dishonest, a section of the audience burst into spontaneous applause while the rest of us froze. It was an astonishing moment. Worship of the Golden Calf, though general in the free world, is ritually decried; yet here were worshipers flaunting their adoration of that brazen god.

The production is good enough. Melvyn Douglas is often touching as the bewildered President. (That is a real theme, by the way: the puzzled man thrust into a world he does not comprehend: "I'm not an expert in this but I think, uh, maybe . . ." After the last seven years any of us could make something out of that.) If I have any quarrel with Mr. Douglas's characterization, it is the laugh. One of the faults (or perhaps it is a virtue) of the Commercialites is that they do not take their characters from life but from other commercial plays. Fatuous politicians *always* smoke cigars and laugh genially. Therefore, since he is most fatuous of all, Mr. Douglas must chuckle like a hyena through nearly every phrase. I am sure that even our electorate with its passion for mediocrity would think twice before voting such a cretin into the Presidency.

At no point does the play betray any familiarity with politicians. Mr. Douglas at times seems more like a simpleminded movie star surrounded by conniving agents and producers, somewhat in the manner of *The Big Knife*. The dialogue is all wrong. "Has somebody got a number on Rutherford B. Hayes?" asks an ancient judge in a phrase that is pure 1950 show business — MCA, not the White House. Also, we have one pol address another pol as *"Mr.* Senator," and so on. The one distinguished thing about the production is E. G. Marshall as the Attorney General; he continues to be one of the more satisfying actors of our time. The direction of George Roy Hill, though vague as to milieu, is adequate despite a tendency to get actors in a long, sullen line with nothing to do.

And yet one is grateful to the Commercialites for dealing with politics at all. Though they tell us nothing and though the pleasure they give us is mechanical and calculated, at least they have moved out of the world of small private relations informed by psychoanalysis which in recent years has made so much of our theater boring. The Commercialites are shrewd analysts, forever studying the audience, devising new ways of exploiting the obvious, always on the lookout for a "property" that will "go." The fact that Lawrence and Lee have taken soundings and decided that the audience might accept a political cartoon, neutrally rendered, is a splendid bit of sleuthing and a good omen, even pleasurable! *

[*The Reporter,* November 12, 1959.]

* See Note 4 in the Appendix.

THE COUCH IN THE SHRINE:
DORE SCHARY AND PADDY CHAYEFSKY

GEORGE SANTAYANA once said to me: "I am not a mystic but I can *imagine* what it must be like." To paraphrase the late guest of the Blue Nuns, I did not see Dore Schary's *The Highest Tree* but I can imagine what it must have been like. In a burst of right feeling, Mr. Schary took an urgent theme (ban atomic testing) and fashioned a play to illustrate that theme. Now, I am all for this kind of play, in theory at least. But there are dangers peculiarly inherent in the topical play. For one thing, between the early and the late editions of the morning paper, your theme may find itself resolved by careless parliaments, and what you have so eloquently demanded in three acts may have come to pass offstage. Between the conception and the production of Mr. Schary's play fell an unexpected shadow: atomic tests *were* suspended. Yet Mr. Schary persisted, no doubt changing lines here and there to accommodate history: We must not allow these tests to start up again . . . something on that order, inevitably less urgent. A further danger, of course, is that any play that sets out to make a single point which can be stated in a phrase or slogan is not apt to be very interesting to an audience. Those who are in favor of more atomic tests are not going to be swayed by Mr. Schary's partisanship, while the rest of us (apparently a majority) do not need to be stiffened in our conviction by anyone's dramaturgy.

One way Mr. Schary might have made his point would have been to write a very sly play about a solipsistic scientist who, when he finds that he has leukemia (Mr. Schary's scientist's disease), wants everyone else to die, too. He should be eloquent, plausible; at the end of the second act he must have a splendid vision of this great green lovely world cleansed of all humanity — no trace of corrupt man anywhere on earth, save for a quantity of glowing bones. Now there's a play I *would* have gone to see.

If there are no third acts in American life, there are even fewer third acts in our theater. Popular writers have a difficult time facing the consequences of what they have set in motion. To state the truth as a conscientious writer sees it or as the play's own internal logic dictates is usually unpalatable. To me, William Inge's *The Dark at the Top of the Stairs* began rather than ended when husband and wife went upstairs:

clearly that marriage was devised, if not in hell, in a sad limbo; and I found myself curious about what was going to happen next to the stair climbers. I had much the same response to Paddy Chayefsky's *The Tenth Man.*

My admiration for Mr. Chayefsky, though real, knows certain bounds. It seems to me that in nearly every work of his I have seen he manages to evade or compromise the reality his art has made us believe in. *The Bachelor Party*, in many ways his most interesting work, goes quite false at the end when the boy returns gratefully to a prison whose bars are the arms of an unloved, loving wife. I am sure Mr. Chayefsky would say that the ending was truthful and that most of us do not choose freedom but learn to love our cages or at least accept captivity *faute de mieux;* but though this is true it is bitter, and to gloss over the bitterness with sentimentality is dishonest.

There is a superstition in the popular arts that the public will not sit still for an ending that gives them no hope. As with most popular wisdom, there is an element of truth in this. I could imagine no American making a movie as black as Clouzot's *The Wages of Fear*, say, or Bergman's *The Seventh Seal,* to name two films that have dealt with the obvious tragedy inherent in our situation. Americans, having achieved so much material comfort in life, refuse to acknowledge the *Totentanz* we are all engaged in. The result has been a popular (and sometimes serious) art of the most superficial kind. Having dismissed Mind as undemocratic and unfriendly, an American devoted to pleasure has turned almost exclusively to the idea of Love as the only thing worth achieving in the sight of a nonhuman eternity that dismays and chills. We have made the orgasm God, and D. H. Lawrence would have been proud of us, though dismayed perhaps by the fatuity of our panegyrics. I suspect one of the reasons our culture has gone silly with boredom has been its refusal to recognize the inadequacy of Love as a god. Most cultures have had a pantheon; ours has but a single shrine, with a couch in it.

Mr. Chayefsky's virtues are all his own. His faults he shares with the popular art of his time. *The Tenth Man* is a clever and charming theater piece, well staged and well acted, and yet its conclusion is pat, sentimental and familiar. The young man does not believe in God or dybbuks; worst of all, he cannot love. The girl is schizophrenic, but she loves. No particular object in mind, just loves. After an exorcism ceremony in a synagogue, he, not she, is divested of the demon of nonfeeling. Now he can love the girl, and off they go together. As someone said very beautifully, in the argot of Broadway: "The rocks in his head fit the holes in hers."

I didn't believe a word of it. Nor did I much care what became of the lovers, despite a fine performance by Donald Harron. Theatrically, the evening belongs to the other nine men and the young rabbi. I don't recall having seen a play in which so many minor characters were so effectively brought to life and with such economy. Mr. Chayefsky is a curious phenomenon. He is a writer with a first-rate imagination; he is already a master of the theater (and may I remind the serious-minded that this is not a trivial accomplishment?); yet he is as completely a victim of the prejudices and received opinion of our society as the most conscienceless writer of half-hour television plays. It is a pity, because with his gifts he could very easily be a useful and revelatory playwright.

[The *Reporter*, December 10, 1959.]

STRANGERS AT BREAKFAST:
"FIVE FINGER EXERCISE"

THE FIRST SCENE of Peter Shaffer's *Five Finger Exercise* is as depressing a bit of playwriting as one will ever encounter, even in the British theater where cozy domesticity and blandness enjoy much the same esteem as the Queen, and for much the same reason. The family trots onstage at breakfast (plays and novels by inexperienced writers almost always start in the morning; I give that small insight to the graduate schools to do with as they will). And what a family Mr. Shaffer has sketched with his bold crayon! Father has made himself a small fortune manufacturing ugly furniture (I thought some of it was in use in their own house, but apparently the pieces on view during the evening are meant to be awfully good; I'm not sure whether this is Mr. Shaffer's irony or the set designer's irony at Mr. Shaffer's expense). The father has a genial contempt for culture and fine manners, a geniality that tends to turn ugly if pressed. Mum is a culture snob, trying to get above her station both intellectually and socially. She uses French phrases and misquotations, and generally behaves as though she might at any moment have to depend almost entirely upon the kindness of strangers. The son talks and talks and talks in the current British manner for the young. After two centuries of reticence the British male has finally found his tongue, and I doubt if he will ever stop talking again. I suppose that when he was Out There building an empire and solemnly mismanaging the affairs of lesser breeds, it was a good idea for him to speak only in strangled monosyllables, on the very wise assumption that if he talked freely he might betray ignorance and lack of sympathy. But now that the Raj has flown and the banners have been furled (who among us will forget John Osborne's threnody in *Look Back in Anger* to the last trooping of the colors Out There?), the British male, restricted to a small island, has suddenly, with a roar of relief, discarded the phlegmatic image (as the advertisers say) of two centuries and turned into a chattering, rather happy fellow (Oh, there are Things Wrong, but once you talk about them it helps, doesn't it?). And in a few years' time I am sure he will even be able to burst into song without provocation, becoming the Neapolitan of the North Sea. Meanwhile, he is just very, very articulate.

Yet Mr. Shaffer's boy is of a more engaging sort than

one usually encounters in the current English theater. He is just starting at Cambridge. He has a little fantasy life with his mother in which she is the Empress of Russia (Catherine, I think) and he is a Cossack admirer. For a moment in the first scene I experienced a sudden evil hope that that ultimate incest-drama writers have been alluding to more and more openly might at long last explode upon the audience, with mother and son at the end going off together to find a new life without Dad. But Mr. Shaffer is up to other things, which I shall come to in a moment. To complete this family of stereotypes, there is the young girl who speaks with outrageous sophistication and wit and aplomb, but is really nice and a virgin and a decent girl. Apparently the late F. Hugh Herbert did not break the mold when he departed this life; she belongs to us all now.

The narrative is as simple as the characterizations. A German tutor is engaged for the young girl. He is a youth of great innocence, a Teutonic Billy Budd, cast among selfish domestic mariners. The mother, the son, the daughter each in turn is attracted to him. Each wants him for his own. He declines to give himself exclusively to any one of them, partly through policy, partly through plain inadequacy in dealing with such bald hungers. The mother tousles his hair on a sofa; the son sees her; the son gets drunk and tells the father, making the matter worse in the telling. The mother tries to go beyond maternal hair tousling only to find the tutor has indeed been drawn to her — but in a filial, not a sexual, way. The mother becomes an enemy. Charges and countercharges are made. The tutor is fired and the father threatens to have him deported to hated Germany. The tutor attempts suicide and fails, and the curtain falls with everyone a bit more alive than at the beginning.

Out of this unpromising material Mr. Shaffer has made a good play, and it is interesting to speculate on how he managed it. What makes this flat little tale work is, I think, the implicit comment that is made on the family. The family is shown here as an impossible sterile fact of society. Four strangers with nothing in common are forced by ties of blood (and economy) to share the same house. We know that at the first opportunity each will detach from the others: the daughter into marriage, the son into homosexuality, the mother into her own dream world (hers is the tragedy, for she is truly useless and knows it), the father into his work and the dim companionship of his peers. Though Mr. Shaffer makes nothing of it, I could not help but feel that this was the first anti-family play since Strindberg. I mean "anti" in the sense that there is no alternative to the unhappy family except nonfamily.

It is possible Mr. Shaffer did not recognize his theme. Yet it is a great one, and he is to be congratulated for having, if only by implication, dramatized it. For he suggests, and I think it is a fact (which will of course be much disputed, as facts usually are), that the family in the West is finished. The family as we know it has evolved over the millennia, from the tribes of pre-history; and its origin was economic, not biological. Yet once a woman can support herself in society and bring up her children by herself, and once there are sufficient jobs, scholarships, and economic opportunities for the young, then the patriarchal system is at an end; the odd group of strangers that make up every family no longer have any reason to live together, to suffer from one another's jagged edges.

But the human race is nothing if not reactionary in its tribal codes, and we do our best to create as much guilt and confusion as we can in those who transgress ancient law. Nevertheless, at some point reality must intrude. In all highly organized urban civilizations, past and present, the family has disintegrated, and instead of crying decadence, society might be wiser to reconsider the actual needs of human beings, to realize that there is a profound difference between the city dweller of Rome (A.D. 200) or New York City (A.D. 1960) and the savage tribesmen in Judea or Thessaly whose economic needs and religious superstitions we still pretend to judge ourself by.*

[The *Reporter*, January 7, 1960.]

* See Note 5 in the Appendix.

BOOKS

LADDERS TO HEAVEN:
NOVELISTS AND CRITICS OF THE 1940'S

I T IS A RARE and lucky physician who can predict accurately at birth whether a child is to become a dwarf or a giant or an ordinary adult, since most babies look alike and the curious arrangements of chromosomes which govern stature are inscrutable and do not yield their secret order even to the shrewdest eye. Time alone gives definition. Nevertheless, interested readers and writers, like anxious parents and midwives, forever speculate upon the direction and meaning of current literary trends, and professional commentators with grave authority make analyses which the briefest interval often declares invalid. But despite their long historic record of bad guesses, bookish men continue to make judgments, and the recorded derelictions of taste and the erratic judgments of earlier times tend only to confirm in them a sense of complacency: *they* are not we, and did not know; *we* know. To disturb this complacency is occasionally worthwhile, and one way of doing it is to exhume significant critical texts from the recent past. Those of the last century, in particular, provide us with fine warnings.

For instance: "We do not believe any good end is to be effected by fictions which fill the mind with details of imaginary vice and distress and crime, or which teach it instead of endeavoring after the fulfillment of simple and ordinary duty to aim at the assurance of superiority by creating for itself fanciful and incomprehensible perplexities. Rather we believe that the effect of such fictions tends to render those who fall under their influence unfit for practical exertion by intruding on minds which ought to be guarded from impurity the unnecessary knowledge of evil." This was the *Quarterly Review* on George Eliot's *The Mill on the Floss,* and it is really quite well said: the perennial complaint of the professional reviewers and the governors of lending libraries ("enough unpleasant things in the world without reading about them in books").

Or the following attack on preciosity and obscurantism (*Blackwood's Magazine,* 1817): "Mr. Coleridge conceives himself to be a far greater man than the public is likely to admit; and we wish to waken him from what seems to us a most ludicrous delusion. He seems to believe that every tongue is wagging in his praise. . . . The truth is that Mr. Coleridge is but an obscure name in English literature [Coleridge was forty-five years old at this time and his major work was long since done]. In London he is well known in literary society for his extraordinary loquacity . . ." And there follows a prolix attack upon the *Biographia Literaria.*

Or this excerpt from an 1848 *Quarterly Review,* deploring the pagan, the sexual, and the vicious:

At all events there can be no interest attached to the writer of *Wuthering Heights* — a novel succeeding *Jane Eyre* and purporting to be written by Ellis Bell — unless it were for the sake of more individual reprobation. For though there is a decided resemblance between the two, yet the aspect of the Jane and Rochester animals in their native state, as Catherine and Heatfield [*sic*], is too odiously and abominably pagan to be palatable even to the most vitiated class of English readers. With all the unscrupulousness of the French school of novels it combines that repulsive vulgarity in the choice of its vice which supplies its own antidote.

Differently worded, these complaints still sound in our press. The Luce editors who cry for an "affirmative" literature echo voices once raised against George Eliot. When middlebrow reviewers deplore "morbidity" in our best writers, they only paraphrase the outrage of those who found the Brontës repellent. And the twitterings of an Orville Prescott when he has discovered a nice and busy book trill the same homely song of those long-dead reviewers who found in the three-volume novels of forgotten lady writers so much warm comfort.

As the essential problems of life remain the same from generation to generation, despite altered conditions, so the problems of literary recognition remain, for contemporaries, peculiarly difficult. Despite the warnings of other times, the impetuous and the confident continue their indiscriminate cultivation of weeds at the expense of occasional flowers.

To consider the writing of any period, including the present, it is perhaps of some importance to examine the climate in which the work is done, to chart if possible the prevailing winds, the weather of the day.

Today there is a significant distinction between the reviewers for popular newspapers and magazines, whom no one interested in literature reads, and the serious critics of the Academy, who write for one another in the quarterlies and, occasionally, for the public in the Sunday supplements. The reviewers are not sufficiently relevant or important to be considered in any but a social sense: they reflect the commonest prejudices and aspirations of the middle class for whom they write, and they need not concern us here.

The critics, however, are more significant. They are dedicated men; they are serious; their learning is often respectable. They have turned to the analysis of literature with the same intensity that, born in an earlier time, they might have brought to formal philosophy, to the law, to the ministry. They tend, generically and inevitably, to be absolutists. They believe that by a close examination of "the text," the laws and the crafty "strategies" of its composition will be made clear and the findings will provide "touchstones" for a comparative criticism of other works. So far so good. They have constructed some ingenious and perhaps valuable analyses of metaphysical verse whose order is often precise and whose most disparate images proceed with a calculable wit and logic.

Unfortunately, the novel is not so easily explicated. It is a loose form, and although there is an inherent logic in those books we are accustomed to call great, the deducible laws which governed the execution of *Emma* are not going to be of much use in defining *The Idiot.* The best that a serious analyst can hope to do is comment intelligently from his vantage point in time on the way a work appears to him in a contemporary, a comparative, or a historic light; in which case his opinion is no more valuable than his own subtlety and knowledge. He must be, as T. S. Eliot put it so demurely, "very intelligent." The point, finally, is that he is not an empiricist dealing with measurable quantities and calculable powers. Rather, he is a man dealing with the private vision of another, with a substance as elusive and amorphous as life itself. To *pretend* that there are absolutes is necessary in making relative judgments (Faulkner writes better than Taylor Caldwell), but to *believe* that there are absolutes and to order one's judgments accordingly is folly and disastrous. One is reminded of Matthew Arnold

and his touchstones; it was his conviction that certain
lines from a poet by all conceded great might be compared to those of lesser poets to determine their value.
Arnold selected Dante as his great poet, an irreproacha-
ble choice, but then he misread the Italian, which naturally caused some confusion. Arnold's heirs also demand order, tidiness, labels, ultimate assurance that
this work is "good" and that work is "bad," but sooner or
later someone misreads the Italian and the system
breaks down. In our time there are nearly as many critical systems as there are major critics, which is a pleasing
anarchy. The "new critics," as they have been called
(*they* at least dislike being labeled and few will now
answer to the title "new critic"), are fundamentally me-
chanics. They go about dismantling the text with the
same rapture that their simpler brothers experience
while taking apart combustion engines: inveterate tink-
erers both, solemnly playing with what has been invented by others for use, not analysis.

Today's quarterlies are largely house organs for
the academic world. They seldom publish imaginative
work and one of their most distinguished editors has
declared himself more interested in commentaries on
writing than in the writing itself. Their quarrels and
schisms and heresies do not in the least resemble the
Alexandrians whom they occasionally mention, with in-
voluted pride, as spiritual ancestors. Rather, one is reminded of the semantic and doctrinal quarrels of the
church fathers in the fourth century, when a diphthong

was able to break the civilized world in half and spin civilization into nearly a millennium of darkness. One could invent a most agreeable game of drawing analogies between the fourth century and today: F. R. Leavis and Saint Jerome are perfectly matched, while John Chrysostom and John Crowe Ransom suggest a possibility. The analogy works amusingly on all levels save one: the church fathers had a Christ to provide them with a primary source of revelation, while our own dogmatists must depend either upon private systems or else upon those proposed by such slender reeds as Matthew Arnold and T. S. Eliot, each, despite his genius, a ritual victim as well as a hero of literary fashion.

But the critics are indefatigable and their game is in earnest, for it is deeply involved not only with literature but with such concrete things as careers in the Academy where frequent and prestigious publication is important. Yet for all their busyness they are by no means eclectic: in a Henry James year not one will write an analysis of George Meredith. They tend to ignore the contemporary writers, not advancing much later than F. Scott Fitzgerald, whose chief attraction is that he exploded before he could be great, providing a grim lesson in failure that, in its completeness, must be awfully heartening when contemplated on the safe green campus of some secluded school.

Of the critics today, Edmund Wilson, the most interesting and the most important, has shown virtually no interest in the writing of the last fifteen years, his talents

engaged elsewhere in the construction of heroic sepul-
chers for old friends like Fitzgerald and Millay, a likable
loyalty but a not entirely useful one. He can of course
still make a fine point during a Peacock flurry and he has
been startlingly brilliant in recent essays on Grant and
Lincoln, but one can search the pages of that book of his
which he calls a "Literary Chronicle of the Forties"
without coming upon any but the most cursory mention
of the decade's chief talents.

Malcolm Cowley, a good professional literary man,
had some sharp things to say recently about the young
writers. Although he made almost no reference to the
better writing of the day, he did say some accurate
things about the university-trained writers, whose work,
he feels, is done with too reverent an eye upon their old
teachers, the new critics. Cowley speaks out for a hearty
freedom from university influence, citing his own generation (the men of the 1920's are loyal to their time if not
to one another: *everyone* was a genius then, and liquor
was cheap abroad) as being singularly independent of
formal instruction. Yet McCullers, Bowles, Capote, etc.
(like Hemingway, Faulkner, O'Neill, etc.) are not grad-
uates of universities, and many of the other young
lions have had enough war to wash them clean of aca-
demicism. Mr. Cowley, like most commentators, tends to
bend whatever he finds to his premise. To him there is
no single genius who can set the tone for a generation
but one wonders if he would recognize that great writer
any more than Lord Jeffrey, a century ago, was able to

recognize *his* time's greatness? For the Cowleys, the novel stopped at *Gatsby*. That Carson McCullers (whom he does not mention) has influenced many works, that Tennessee Williams has influenced the theater of the world, that Paul Bowles, among others, has reshaped the short story — none of these things impinges on him.

Mr. Cowley's gloom is supported by a younger critic, John Aldridge, whose approach, though societal rather than aesthetic, is interesting. He betrayed his fundamental confusion, however, when in his amusing novel *After the Lost Generation* he got onto the subject of "values" (by way of Lionel Trilling and perhaps V. S. Pritchett). He discussed a number of fictitious characters who were writing books (using real, if unlikely, names like Truman Capote and Gore Vidal) and he proved, by the evidence of their works, that they had all failed of greatness because, except for "a pocket or two of manners" (the Army; the South; here and there in New England), there was really nothing left to write about, none of that social conflict out of which comes art, like sparks from a stone grinding metal. His coda indicated that a young writer of singular genius is at this moment hovering in the wings awaiting his cue. It will be interesting to read Mr. Aldridge's next novel.

Yet Mr. Aldridge does have a case: the old authority of church, of settled Puritan morality, *has* broken down, and if one's vision is historically limited to only a few generations in time it might seem that today's novelists are not having the fun their predecessors in the 1920's had, breaking cultural furniture. But to take a longer view, one must recall that the great times for literature and life were those of transition: from the Middle Ages to modern times by way of the Renaissance, from dying paganism to militant Christianity by way of the Antonines, and so on back to Greece. The opportunity for the novelist when Mr. Aldridge's "values" are in the discard is fabulous: to create without wasting one's substance in political or social opposition. What could be more marvelous! Neither Vergil nor Shakespeare had to attack their day's morality or those in authority. They were morally free to write of life, of Henry James's "the main thing." There were certainly inequities and barbarities in sixteenth-century England and first-century Rome, but the writers, affected partly by convention (and even by the Star Chamber), did not address themselves to attacks upon the government or the time's morality, which, apparently, did not obsess them. Writers, after all, are valuable in spite of their neuroses, obsessions, and rebellions, not because of them. It is a poor period indeed which must assess its men of letters in terms of their opposition to their society. Opposition to life's essential conditions perhaps, or to death's implacable tyranny, is something else again, and universal; but novels, no matter how clever, which attempt to change statutes or moral attitudes are, though useful at the moment, not literature at all. In fact, if Mr. Aldridge were right in his proposition we would have *not* a barren, "subjectless" world for literature but the exact opposite: a time of flowering, of creation without waste and irrelevancy. Unhappily, American society has not changed that much in the last thirty years: there is as much to satirize, as much to protest as ever before, and it will always be the task of the secondary figures to create those useful public books whose momentary effect is as stunning as their literary value is not.

There is no doubt but that the West has come to Malraux's "twilight of the absolute." One awaits with hope the period between when, unencumbered by the junk of dogma, writers can turn to the great things with confidence and delight. Loss of authority by removing targets does not destroy the true novelist, though it eliminates the doctrinaire and those busy critics who use the peculiar yardstick of social usefulness to determine merit. (It is no accident that the few works admired by Mr. Aldridge are those compositions which sturdily and loudly discuss the social scene, or some "pocket" of it — interesting books, certainly, whose public effect is often admirable; though the noise they create seldom persists long enough to enjoy even a first echo.) Actually, one might say that it is only the critic who suffers unduly from the lack of authority. A critic, to criticize, must, very simply, have standards. To have standards he must pretend there is some optimum against which like creations can be measured. By the nature of his own process he is eventually forced, often inadvertently, to accept as absolute those conditions for analysis which he has only tentatively proposed. To be himself significant he needs law and revealed order; without them he is only a civilized man commenting for others upon given works which, temperamentally, he may or may not like without altering the value, if any, of the work examined. With a law, with authority, with faith he becomes something more grand and meaningful; the pythoness through whom passes Apollo's word.

Much of the despondency and apparent confusion in the world of peripheral letters today derives partly from the nervous, bloody age in which we live and partly from that hunger for the absolute which, in our own immediate experience, delivered two great nations into the hands of tyrants, while in our own country the terror of being man alone, unsupported by a general religious belief and undirected by central authority, has reduced many intellectuals either to a bleak nihilism or, worse, to the acceptance of some external authority (Rome, Marx, Freud). One is reminded of Flaubert's comment nearly a century ago: "The melancholy of the ancients seems to me deeper than that of the moderns, who all more or less assume an immortality on the far side of the black pit. For the ancients the black pit was infinity itself; their dreams take shape and pass against a background of unchanging ebony. No cries, no struggles, only the fixity of the pensive gaze. The gods being dead and Christ not yet born [sic], there was between

Cicero and Marcus Aurelius one unique moment in which there was man."

Our own age is one of man alone, but there are still cries, still struggles against our condition, against the knowledge that our works and days have value only in the human scale; and those who most clearly remember the secure authority of other times, the ordered universe, the immutable moral hierarchies, are the ones who most protest the black pit. While it is perfectly true that any instant in human history is one of transition, ours more than most seems to be marked by a startling variety of conflicting absolutes, none sufficiently great at this moment to impose itself upon the majority whose lives are acted out within an unhuman universe which some still prefer to fill with a vast manlike shadow containing stars, while others behold only a luminous dust which *is* stars, and us as well. This division between those who recognize the unhumanity of creation and those who protest the unchanging ebony sets the tone of our literature, with the imaginative writers inclining (each in his own way) to the first view and their critics to the second. The sense of man not being king of creation (nor even the work of a king of creation) is the burden, directly and indirectly, of modern literature. For the writers there is no reality for man except in his relations with his own kind. Much of the stuff of earlier centuries — like fate, high tragedy, the interventions of *dei ex machina* — have been discarded as brave but outworn devices, not applicable to a world where kings and commoners occupy the same sinking boat.

Those of our writers who might yet enjoy the adjective "affirmative" are the ones who tend to devote themselves to the dramas within the boat, the encompassing cold sea ignored in the passions of the human moment. Most of the worst and a number of the best writers belong to this category. The key words here are "love" and "compassion." And though, like most such devices, they have grown indistinct with use, one can still see them at work and marvelously so, in the novels of Carson Mc-Cullers and certain (though not all) of the plays of Tennessee Williams. Christopher Isherwood once said that to his mind the finest single line in modern letters was: "I have always depended upon the kindness of strangers," from *A Streetcar Named Desire*. At such moments, in such works, the human drama becomes so unbearably intense that time and the sea are blotted out and only the human beings are illuminated as they cease, through the high magic of art, to be mere residents in a time which stops and become, instead, archetypes — elemental figures like those wild gods our ancestors peopled heaven with.

Then there are the writers to whom neither sea nor boat exists. They have accepted some huge fantasy wherein they need never drown, where death is life, and the doings of human beings on a social and ethical level are of much consequence to some brooding source of creation who dispenses his justice along strictly party

lines at the end of a gloomy day. To this category belong
such talented writers as Graham Greene and Evelyn
Waugh. In theory at least, speculation has ended for
them; dogma supports them in all things. Yet it is odd to
find that the tone of their works differs very little from
that of the other mariners adrift. They are, if anything,
perhaps a bit more lugubrious, since for them is not the
principality of this world.

Finally, there are those who see human lives as the
lunatic workings of compulsive animals no sooner born
than dead, no sooner dead than replaced by similar
creatures born of that proliferating seed which too will
die. Paul Bowles is a striking example of this sort of
writer as he coolly creates nightmare visions in which
his specimens struggle and drown in fantasy, in madness, in death. His short stories with their plain lines of
monochromatic prose exploit extreme situations with a
chilling resourcefulness; he says, in short, "Let it sink;
let us drown."

Carson McCullers, Paul Bowles, Tennessee Williams
are, at this moment at least, the three most interesting
writers in the United States. Each is engaged in the
task of truth-saying (as opposed to saying the truth,
which is not possible this side of revelation). Each
has gone further into the rich interior of the human
drama than any of our immediate predecessors with the
possible exception of William Faulkner, whose recent
work has unfortunately resembled bad translations
from Pindar. On a social level, the hostility shown these

essential artists is more significant than their occasional worldly successes, for it is traditional that he who attempts to define man's condition demoralizes the majority, whether relativist or absolutist. We do not want ever to hear that we will die but that first we must live; and those ways of living which are the fullest, the most intense, are the very ones which social man traditionally dreads, summoning all his superstition and malice to combat strangers and lovers, the eternal victims.

The obsessive concern with sexuality which informs most contemporary writing is not entirely the result of a wish *épater le bourgeois* but, more, the reflection of a serious battle between the society man has constructed so illogically and confusedly and the nature of the human being, which needs a considerably fuller expression sexually and emotionally than either the economics or morality of this time will permit. The sea is close. Two may find the interval between awareness and death more meaningful than one alone. Yet while ours is a society where mass murder and violence are perfectly ordinary and their expression in the most popular novels and comic books is accepted with aplomb, any love between two people which does not conform is attacked.

Malcolm Cowley has complained that writers no longer handle some of the more interesting social relationships of man, that there is no good stock-market novel, no Balzacian concern among the better writers with economic motive. His point is valid. The public range of the novel has been narrowed. It would be good to have well-written accounts of the way we live now, yet our important writers eschew, almost deliberately it would seem, the kind of book which provided not only Trollope but Tolstoi with so much power. Mr. Cowley catches quite well the tone of the second-rate good writers (a phenomenon peculiar to this moment: it seems as if a whole generation writes well, though not often to any point); they are concerned with the small scale, and goodness as exemplified by characters resembling the actress Shirley Booth holding out valiantly against villainous forces, usually represented by someone in business. But Mr. Cowley does not mention the novelist from whom these apotheosis-in-the-kitchen writers derive. Carson McCullers, using the small scale, the relations of human beings at their most ordinary, transcends her milieu and shows, in bright glimpses, the potentiality which exists in even the most banal of human relationships, the "we" as opposed to the meager "I."

Or again, in Tennessee Williams's remarkable play *Camino Real,* though the world is shown in a nightmare glass, a vision of those already drowned, there are still moments of private triumphs . . . in Kilroy's love with (not for) the gypsy's daughter and in Lord Byron's proud departure through the gate to *terra incognita,* his last words a reproach and an exhortation: "Make voyages! Make voyages!"

And, finally, most starkly, we have a deliberate act of murder, Gide's *l'acte gratuite,* which occurs at the end of Paul Bowles's *Let It Come Down*. Here the faceless, directionless protagonist, in a sudden storm of rage against his life, all life, commits a murder without reason or passion, and in this one terrible moment (similar perhaps to that of a nation gone to war) he at last finds "a place in the world, a definite status, a precise relationship with the rest of men. Even if it had to be one of open hostility, it was his, created by him." In each of these three writers man acts, through love, through hate, through despair. Though the act in each is different, the common emotion is sufficiently intense to dispel, for a time at least, the knowledge of that cold drowning which awaits us all.

The malady of civilized man is his knowledge of death. The good artist, like the wise man, addresses himself to life and invests with his private vision the deeds and thoughts of men. The creation of a work of art, like an act of love, is our one small "yes" at the center of a vast "no."

The lesser writers whose works do not impress Mr. Cowley despite their correctness possess the same vision as those of the major writers, but their power of illusion is not so great and their magic is only fitful: too often their creatures are only automatons acted upon. Though they may shed light on interesting aspects of ordinary life they do not, in the best sense, illuminate, flood with brilliance, our strange estate.

Among the distinguished second rank of younger writers there is much virtuosity and potentiality. The coolly observant short stories of Louis Auchincloss provide wise social comment of the sort which the Cowleys would probably admire but never seem to read in their haste to generalize. Eudora Welty fashions a subtle line and Jean Stafford, though currently obsessed with literary interior decoration, has in such stories as "The Echo and the Nemesis" displayed a talent which makes all the more irritating her recent catalogues of bric-a-brac, actual and symbolic. John Kelly, whose two novels have been neglected, has created a perverse, operatic world like nothing else in our literature, while the late John Horne Burns, out of fashion for some years, was a brilliant satirist in a time when satire is necessary but difficult to write since to attack successfully one must have a complacent, massive enemy — and though there are numerous villains today, none is entirely complacent.

The serious writers have been attacked by the reviewers for their contempt of narrative and their neglect to fashion "real live characters" (which means familiar stereotypes from Victorian fiction masquerading in contemporary clothes). The reviewers have recognized that a good deal of writing now being done doesn't resemble anything they are used to (although in almost a century there has been a royal line of which they are ignorant . . . from *The Temptation of Saint Anthony* to *The Golden Bowl* to *Mrs. Dalloway*); they still feel most at home with *The Newcomes,* or, if they came to maturity in the 1920's, with *The Sun Also Rises.* When the technique of a play like *Camino Real* seems bizarre and difficult to follow for those accustomed to the imitators of Ibsen, there must be a genuine reason for the change in technique, other than the author's presumed perversity. The change from the exterior to the interior world which has been taking place in literature for at least a century is due not only to a general dissatisfaction with the limitations of naturalism but also to the rise of a new medium, the movies, which, properly used, are infinitely superior to the old novel and to the naturalistic play, especially in the rendering of plain narrative.

The Quiet One, a movie, was far superior as a social document (as "art," too, for that matter) to any book published so far in this country dealing with Negro problems. Instinctively, the writers have reacted to the camera. If another medium can handle narrative and social comment so skillfully, even on their lowest aesthetic levels, then the novelist must go deeper, must turn into the maze of consciousness where the camera cannot follow. He must also become wise, and wisdom even in its relative sense was never a notable characteristic of novelists in our language. One can anticipate the direction of the novel by studying that of the painters who, about the time of the still camera's invention, began instinctively to withdraw into a less literal world where they might do work which a machine could not imitate. It is a possibility, perhaps even a probability, that as the novel moves toward a purer, more private expression it will cease altogether to be a popular medium, becoming, like poetry, a cloistered avocation — in which case those who in earlier times might have written great public novels will be engaged to write good public movies, redressing the balance. In our language the novel is but three centuries old and its absorption by the movies, at least the vulgar line of it, is not necessarily a bad thing. In any event, it is already happening.

For the present, however, the tone of the contemporary novel, though not cheerful, is precise. Man is on his own. In certain human actions, in love, in violence, he can communicate with others, touch and be touched, act and in the act forget his fate. The scale is often small. Kings are neglected because, to relativists, all men are the same within eternity. Or rather their crisis is the same. The concern in modern letters is with that crisis which defines the prospect.

In general, the novelists have rejected authority, parting company with their cousins-german the serious critics. To the creative man, religious dogma and political doctrine, when stated in ultimate terms, represent the last enemy, the protean Lucifer in our race's bloody progress. The artist speaks from that awareness of life, that secret knowledge of life in death the absolutists are driven to obscure and to distort, to shape, if possible, to tidy ends.

The interior drama at its most bitterly human comes into sharp focus in the writings of Williams and Mc-Cullers, and there are signs that other writers, undismayed by the hostility of the absolutists, may soon provide us with some strength in these last days before the

145

sure if temporary victory of that authoritarian society which, thanks to science, now has every weapon with which to make even the most inspired lover of freedom conform to the official madness.

The thought of heaven, a perennial state of mind, a cheerful conception of what might be in life, in art (if not in death), may yet save our suicidally inclined race — if only because heaven is as various as there are men in the world who dream of it, and writers to evoke that dream. One recalls Constantine (to refer again to the image of the early church) when he teased a dissenting bishop at one of the synods: "Acesius, take a ladder and get up to heaven by yourself." We are fortunate in our time to have so many ladders going up. Each ladder is raised in hope, which is heaven enough.

[*New World Writing* #4, 1953.]

A NOTE ON THE NOVEL

Any DISCUSSION of the novel nowadays soon strikes the pessimistic note. It is agreed, for instance, that there are among us no novelists of sufficient importance to act as touchstones for useful judgment. There is Faulkner, but . . . and there is Hemingway, but . . . And that completes the list of near-misses, the others, poor lost legions, all drowned in the culture's soft buzz and murmur. We have embarked upon empire (Rome born again our heavy fate) without a Vergil in the crew, only tarnished silver writers in a bright uranium age, perfunctorily divided by editorialists between the "affirmative" (and good) and the "negative" (and bad). Only cultural researchers (wandering lonely as a crowd) and high critics merit serious attention. From the little red schoolhouse to the library at Alexandria in one generation is the heartening success story of American letters.

Apologists (secret lovers of the novel, few but tender) surveying the seasonal flood of first novels of promise, the smaller wave of second novels of no promise, and, finally, most poignant of all, those minuscule ripples which continue so perversely to assault an indifferent shore — these apologists have noted a spiritual ergot in our country's air which causes good writers to abort young while, tributary to this new myth, lingers the old conviction that American life, even now, lacks the class tensions, the subtle play of manners (Hialeah but no Ascot), the requisite amount of history to make even a small literature. That from Levittowns no art may come is still an important critical thesis.

One senses, too, in academic dialogues and explications the unstated burden of the discussion that, at last, all the novels are in. The term is over, the canon assembled if not ordered, the door to the library firmly shut to the irrelevance of new attempts. More ominous, however, than the loss of the higher criticism has been the gradual defection of the public itself. After some three hundred years the novel in English has lost the general reader (or rather the general reader has lost the novel), and I propose that he will not again recover his old enthusiasm.

The fault, if it be a fault, is not the novelist's (I doubt if there ever have been so many interesting and excellent writers as there are now working) but of the audience, an unpleasant accusation to make in a democracy where, ultimately, the taste of the majority is the measure of all things. Nevertheless, appalling education combined with clever new toys has distracted that large public which found pleasure in prose fictions. In an odd way, our civilization has now come full circle: from the Greek mysteries and plays to the printing press and the novel to television and plays again, the audience has returned to the play, and it is now clear that the novel, despite its glories, was only surrogate for the drama, which, confined till this era to theaters, was not generally accessible.

With television (ten new "live" plays a week; from such an awful abundance, a dramatic renaissance *must* come) the great audience now has the immediacy it has always craved, the picture which moves and talks, the story experienced, not reported. In refutation, it may indeed be argued that the large sales of paperback books, both good and bad, are proof that there are millions out there in the dark, hungering for literature. But though it is true that all those books must go *somewhere*, I suggest that their public is not a serious one, that it is simply pursuing secret vices from one bright cover picture to another — consuming, not reading.

Yet all in all, this state of affairs, though disheartening, is by no means tragic. For one thing, those novelists whose interests are in polemic or mere narrative will doubtless join the new Establishment and write plays. Adventure stories, exotic voyages, superficial histories, all the familiar accouterments of the popular novel are now the scenarists' by right of conquest. The novel is left only the best things: that exploration of the inner world's divisions and distinctions where no camera may follow, the private, the necessary pursuit of the whole which makes the novel, at its highest, the humane art that Lawrence called "The one bright book of life."

To strike an optimistic note, if faintly, it may well be that, with unpopularity, the meretricious and the ordinary will desert entirely, leaving only the devoted lashed to the mast. But now the tide is in. The course is set. The charts are explicit, for we are not the first to make the voyage out: the poets long ago preceded us into exile, and one can observe them up ahead, arms outstretched to greet the old enemy, their new companions at the austere edge of the known world.*

[*New York Times Book Review*, August 5, 1956.]

* See Note 6 in the Appendix.

THE DEMOTIC NOVEL:
JOHN DOS PASSOS

THERE IS A terrible garrulousness in most American writing, a legacy no doubt of the Old Frontier. But where the more inspired tall-talesmen of simpler days went on and on, never quite certain and never much caring what the next load of breath might contain, at their best they imparted with a new demotic flare the sense of life living. Unfortunately, since these first originals the main line of the American novel has reverted to incontinent heirs, to the gabblers, maunderers, putters-in of everything. Watch: Now the man goes into the barbershop and sees four chairs with two people in them, one with a beard and the other reading a comic book about Bugs Bunny, then the man sits in the chair, he thinks of baby's first curls shorn and (if he's been analyzed) of castration, as he lists for us the labels on every bottle of hair tonic on the shelf, records every word the barber has to say about the Series — all the time wondering what happened to the stiff white brush smelling of stale powder they used to brush the back of your neck with. . . . To get that haircut the true gabbler will devote a dozen pages of random description and dialogue none of which finally has anything to do with his novel's theme, assuming there is one. It was included at that moment because the gabbler happened to think of a visit to a barber, the way good old Tom Wolfe once named all the rivers of America because he felt like it.

For every Scott Fitzgerald concerned with the precise word and the selection of relevant incident, there are a hundred American writers, many well regarded, who appear to believe that one word is just as good as another, and that anything which pops into their heads is worth putting down. It is an attitude unique to us and deriving, I would suspect, from a corrupted idea of democracy: if everything and everyone is of equal value, then any word is as good as any other word to express a meaning, which in turn is no more valuable than any other meaning. Or to put it another way, if everyone is equally valuable, then anything the writer (who is valuable) writes must be of value, so why attempt selection? This sort of writing, which I call demotic, can be observed at its purest in the later work of Jack Kerouac.

One of the better single lines of literary criticism

was made by Thackeray when he said of Smollett, "I fancy he did not invent much." There it all is: the two kinds of writer, underscored by the choice of verb. To fancy. To invent. Most of our writers tend to be recorders. They tell us what happened last summer, why the marriage went wrong, how they lost custody of the children, how much they drank and whom they laid, and if they are demoticists the task of ordering that mass of words and impressions put between covers will be the reader's. Of all the recorders of what happened last summer — or last decade — John Dos Passos is the most dogged. Not since the brothers Goncourt has there been such a dedication to getting down exactly what happened, and were it not for his political passions he might indeed have been a true camera to our time. He invents little; he fancies less. He is often good when he tells you something through which he himself has lived, and noted. He is well equipped to be a good social critic, which is the role he has cast for himself: conscience to the Republic, caveator, stern reminder of good ways lost, of useful ways not taken.

With what seems defiance, the first two pages of John Dos Passos's new novel *Midcentury* are taken up with the titles of his published work, proudly spaced, seventeen titles to the first page, sixteen to the second: thirty-three books, the work of some forty years. The list is testament to Dos Passos's gallantry, to his stubbornness, and to his worldly and artistic failure. To paraphrase Hollywood's harsh wisdom, the persistent writer is only as good as his last decade. Admired extravagantly in the '20's and '30's, Dos Passos was ignored in the '40's and '50's, his new works passed over either in silence or else noted with that ritual sadness we reserve for those whose promise to art was not kept. He himself is aware of his own dilemma, and in a recent novel called *The Great Days* he recorded with brave if bewildered objectivity a decline similar to his own. I shall not try to ring the more obvious changes suggested by his career. Yet I should note that there is something about Dos Passos which makes a fellow writer unexpectedly protective, partly out of compassion for the man himself, and partly because the fate of Dos Passos is a chilling reminder to those condemned to write for life that this is the way it almost always is in a society which, to put it tactfully, has no great interest in the development of its writers, a process too slow for the American temperament. As a result our literature is rich with sprinters but significantly short of milers.

Right off, let me say that unlike most of Dos Passos's more liberal critics, I never cared much for his early work even at its best. On the other hand, I have always enjoyed, even admired, the dottiness of his politics. His political progress from Radical Left to Radical Right seems to me very much in the American grain, and only the most humorless of doctrinaire liberals should be horrified. After all, it is not as if Dos Passos were in any way politically significant. Taken lightly, he gives pleasure. There is a good deal of inadvertent comedy in his admiration for such gorgeous Capitoline geese as Barry Goldwater, while page after page of *Midcentury* is vintage Old Guard demagoguery. For instance there is that old Bourbon comforter "Roosevelt's war" for the Second World War, while, every now and then, a passage seems almost to parody Wisconsin's late wonder:

> Hitler's invasion of the Soviet Union cut off support from the Communists. Stalin needed quick help. Warmonger Roosevelt became the Communists' god. . . . War work meant primarily help for the Soviets to many a Washington bureaucrat.

That "many" is superb. "I have here in my hand a list of MANY Washington bureaucrats who . . ." Politically, to make an atrocious pun, Dos Passos is for the Byrds.

Midcentury is about the American labor movement from, roughly, the New Deal to the present, with occasional reminiscences of earlier times. The form of the book is chaotic. There are prose poems in italics, short impressionistic biographies of actual public figures, several fictional narratives in which various men and women are victimized by labor unions. And of course his patented device from *USA:* using newspaper headlines and fragments of news stories to act as counterpoint to the narration, to give a sense of time and place.

To deal with this last device first. In *USA* it was effective. In that book, Dos Passos stumbled on an interesting truth: nearly all of us are narcotized by newspapers. There is something about the way a newspaper page is set which, if only from habit, holds the attention no matter how boring the matter. Bemused, one reads on, waiting for surprise or titillation. The success of the gossip column is no more than a crude exploitation of newspaper addiction. Even if you don't want to know what the Duchess of Windsor said to Elsa Maxwell or learn what stranger in the night was visited by Sir Stork, if your eye is addicted you will read on numbly.

(Parenthetic note to writers on the make and a warning to exploited readers: any column of text, even this one, will hold the eye and the attention of the reader if there are sufficient familiar proper names. Nat King Cole, Lee Remick, Central Park, Marquis de Sade, Senator Bourke Hickenlooper, Marilyn Monroe. See? I trapped a number of you who'd skimmed the denser paragraphs above, deciding it was pretty dull literary stuff. "Marquis de Sade? Must've skipped something. Let's see, there's 'titillation' . . . no, 'Hollywood' . . . no.")

Also, dialogue has almost the same effect on the eye as names and newspaper headlines. In an age of worsening prose and declining concentration, most readers' attention will wander if there is too much unbroken text. On the other hand, even the most reluctant reader enjoys descending the short sprightly steps of dialogue on the page, jumping the descriptions, to shift the metaphor, as a skilled rider takes hedges in a steeplechase.

The newspaper technique is a good one; but to make it work the excerpts ought, minimally, to have some bearing on the narrative. In *Midcentury* one has the impression that Dos Passos simply shredded a few newspapers at random and stuffed them between the chapters as a form of excelsior to keep the biographies from bumping into one another. On the whole these biographies provide the book with its only interest, although the choice of subjects is inscrutable. Walter Reuther, John L. Lewis, James Hoffa are relevant to a novel dealing with organized labor, but then why include Robert Oppenheimer and Eleanor Roosevelt? And what exactly *is* Sam Goldwyn doing in the book? Or James Dean, that well-known statesman of organized labor? But, disregarding the irrelevance of many of the subjects, Dos Passos handles his impressionistic technique with a good deal of cunning. It is a tribute to his method that I was offended by the job he did on Mrs. Roosevelt. He is wonderfully expert at the precise, low blow. Thus, referring to Oppenheimer's belated political awakening (and turn to the Left): "Perhaps he felt the need to expiate the crime of individuality (as much of a crime to the solid citizens of the American Legion posts as to party functionaries Moscow-trained in revolution)." That's good stuff. He may not make the eagle scream, but he can certainly get the geese to honking. Yet despite his very pretty malice, the real reason the biographies work is again newspaper addiction: we know the subjects already. Our memories round the flat portraits; our prejudices do the author's work.

Finally, we come to the fictional characters, buried beneath headlines, feature stories and prose poems. (*Walking the earth under the stars, musing midnight in midcentury, a man treads the road with his dog; the dog, less timebound in her universe of stench and shrill, trots eager ahead.* . . . Not since Studs Lonigan's old buddy Weary Reilley was making the scene has there been such word-music, I mean wordmusic.) Excepting one, the invented characters are cast in solid cement. Dos Passos tells us this and he tells us that, but he never shows us anything. He is unable to let his characters alone to see which will breathe and which will not. The only story which comes alive is a narrative by a dying labor organizer and onetime Wobbly who recalls his life; and in those moments Dos Passos allows him to hold the stage, one is most moved. If Dos Passos were a novelist instead of a pamphleteer he would have liberated this particular character from the surrounding cement and made a book of him, and in that book, simply told, not only made all his urgent polemical points but art as well. As it is, Dos Passos proves a point well taken by Stendhal: "Politics, amidst the interests of the imagination, are a pistol shot in the middle of a concert. This noise is ear-rending, without being force-ful. It clashes with every instrument."

Dos Passos ends his book with a sudden lashing out at the youth of the day. He drops the labor movement. He examines James Dean. Then he does a Salingeresque first-person narrative of an adolescent who has stolen some credit cards (remember a similar story in *Life?*) and gone on a spree of conspicuous consumption. Despite the confusion of his style, Dos Passos is plain in his indictment: doomed is our pleasure-loving, scorn-ful, empty, flabby modern youth, product of that dream midcentury in which, thanks to the do-gooders, we have lost our ancient Catonian virtue. I found the indictment oddly disgusting. I concede that there is some truth in everything Dos Passos says. But his spirit strikes me as sour and mean and, finally, uncomprehending. To be harsh, he has mistaken the decline of his own flesh and talent for the world's decline. This is the old man's folly, which a good artist or a generous man tries to avoid. Few of us can resist celebrating our own great days or finding fault with those who do not see in us now what we were or might have been. Nor is it un-natural when contemplating extinction to want, in sud-den raging moments, to take the light with one. But it is a sign of wisdom to recognize one's own pettiness and not only to surrender vanity to Death, which means to take it anyway, but to do so with deliberate grace as exemplar to those younger people upon whom our race's fragile continuity, which is all there is, depends.

I should have thought that that was why one wrote —
to make something useful for the survivors, to say: I
was and now you are, and I leave you as good a map as
I could make of my own traveling.

[*Esquire*, May 1961.]

NORMAN MAILER:
THE ANGELS ARE WHITE

I FIRST HEARD of Norman Mailer in the spring of 1948, just before *The Naked and the Dead* was published. He was living in Paris or had been living there and just gone home when I arrived in France, my mood curiously melancholic, no doubt because of the dubious fame I was enjoying with the publication of a third book, *The City and the Pillar*. At twenty-two I should have found a good deal more to please me than I did that spring and summer in the foreign cities. I do recall at one point Truman Capote telling me about *The Naked and the Dead* and its author; a recital which promptly aroused my competitive instincts . . . waning, let me say right off, and for reasons which are relevant to these notes. Yet at that time I remember thinking meanly: So somebody did it. Each previous

161

war had had its big novel, yet so far there had been none for our war, though I knew that a dozen busy friends and acquaintances were grimly taking out tickets in the Grand War Novel Lottery. I had debated doing one myself and had (I still think) done something better: a small cool hard novel about men on the periphery of the action; it was called *Williwaw* and was written when I was nineteen and easily the cleverest young fox ever to know how to disguise his ignorance and make a virtue of his limitations. (What an attractive form the self-advertisement is: one could go on forever relighting one's image!) Not till I began that third book did I begin to get bored with playing safe.

I took to the field and have often wondered since, in the course of many excursions, defeats, alarums and ambushes, what it might have been like to have been a safe shrewd custodian of one's talent, playing from strength. I did not suspect then that the ambitious, rather cold-blooded young contemporary who had set out to write the big war novel and who had pulled it off would one day be in the same fix I was. Not safe. Not wise. Not admired. A fellow victim of the Great Golfer's Age, then no more than a murmur of things to come in the Golfer's murmurous heart.

My first reaction to *The Naked and the Dead* was: it's a fake. A clever, talented, admirably executed fake. I have not changed my opinion of the book since, though I have considerably changed my opinion of

Mailer, as he himself has changed. Now I confess I have never read all of *The Naked and the Dead*. But I read a good deal of it. I recall a fine description of men carrying a dying man down a mountain. Yet every time I got going in the narrative I would find myself stopped cold by a set of made-up, predictable characters taken, not from life, but from the same novels all of us had read, and informed by a naïveté which was at its worst when Mailer went into his Time-Machine and wrote those passages which resemble nothing so much as smudged carbons of an early Dos Passos work.

Sourly, from a distance, that year I watched the fame of Mailer quite surpass John Horne Burns and myself, as well as Truman Capote who had made his debut earlier the same year. I should explain for those who have come in late or were around then but inattentive that the O.K. List of writers in 1947 and 1948 was John Horne Burns, Calder Willingham and myself. Capote and Mailer were added in 1948. Willingham was soon dropped; then Burns (my own favorite) sank, and by 1949 in the aftermath of *The City and the Pillar* I too departed the O.K. List.

"I had the freak of luck to start high on the mountain, and go down sharp while others were passing me" — so Mailer wrote, describing the time after *Barbary Shore* when he unexpectedly joined the rest of us down on the plain. Now the descent, swift or slow, is not agreeable; but on the other hand it is not as tragic as Mailer seems to find it. To be demoralized by the withdrawal of public success (a process as painful in America as the withdrawal of a drug from an addict) is to grant too easily a victory to the society one has attempted to criticize, affect, change, reform. It is clearly unreasonable to expect to be cherished by those one assaults. It is also childish, in the deepest sense of being a child, ever to expect justice. There is none beneath our moon. One can only hope not to be destroyed entirely by injustice and, to put it cynically, one can very often flourish through an injustice obtaining in one's favor. What matters finally is not the world's judgment of oneself but one's own judgment of the world. Any writer who lacks this final arrogance will not survive very long, especially in America.

That wide graveyard of stillborn talents which contains so much of the brief ignoble history of American letters is a tribute to the power of a democracy to destroy its critics, brave fools and passionate men. If there is anything in Mailer's new book which alarms me, it is his obsession with public success. He is running for President, as he puts it. Yet though his best and most interesting works have been unjustly attacked, he should realize that in this most inequitable of worlds his one worldly success was not a very good book, that *The Naked and the Dead* is redolent of "ambition" (in the Mary McCarthy sense of the word — pejorative, needless to say) and a young man's will to be noticed. Mailer himself nearly takes this view: "I may as well confess that by December 8th or 9th of 1941 . . . I was worrying darkly whether it would be more likely that a great war novel would be written about Europe or the Pacific." Ambition and the day coincided and a success was made. Yet it is much less real a book than Burns's *The Gallery*, or even some of the stories of Robert Lowry, works which had the virtue of being felt, possessed entirely by the men who made them, not created out of stern ambition and dogged competence. But, parenthetically, most war books are inadequate. War tends to be too much for any writer, especially one whose personality is already half obliterated by life in a democracy. Even the aristocrat Tolstoi, at a long remove in time, stretched his genius to the breaking point to encompass men and war and the thrust of history in a single vision. Ernest Hemingway in *A Farewell to Arms* did a few good descriptions, but his book, too, is a work of ambition, in which can be seen the beginning of the careful, artful, immaculate idiocy of tone that since has marked both his prose and his legend as he has declined into that sort of fame which, at moments I hope are weak, Mailer seems to crave.

But it is hard for American writers not to measure themselves according to the standards of their time and place. I recall a conversation with Stephen Spender when I lapsed, unconsciously, into the national preoccupation. Some writer had unexpectedly failed, not gone on, blown up. Spender said rather pointedly, "The difference in England is that they *want* us to be

distinguished, to be good." We order things differently;
although our example is contagious, for in recent years
the popular British press has discovered writers in a
way ours never has. Outside the gossip column and the
book page no writer except Hemingway is ever mentioned as news in the American press, but let the most
obscure young English novelist attack the Establishment and there are headlines in London. Mailer can
denounce Eisenhower as much as he likes in *Dissent*
but the readers of the *Daily News* will never know the
name of Mailer, much less the quality of his anger.
Publicity for the American writer is of the "personality" kind: a photograph in *Harper's Bazaar*, bland
television appearances . . . the writer as minor movie
star, and as unheeded.

Mailer and I finally met in 1954. I had just published
my last, or perhaps I should say latest, novel, *Messiah*,
and it had sunk quietly into oblivion in America. (If
it were not for the continuing interest of Europe, especially England, a great many of our writers would
not survive as well as they do their various seasons of
neglect.) I liked Mailer, though I am afraid my first
impression of him was somewhat guarded. I am suspicious of people who make speeches at me, and he is a
born cocktail-party orator. I have not the slightest rec-
ollection of what we talked about. I do recall telling
him that I admired *Barbary Shore*, and he was shrewd
enough to observe that probably I had been driven to
read it to see if it was really as bad as everyone thought.

Which it was not. Of his three novels I find it the most interesting and the least diffuse, and quite literally memorable. It is hallucinatory writing of a kind Mailer tried, as far as I know, only that one time; and though I think his talents are essentially naturalistic, he does seem again in his new novel (judging from the advance samples he displays in *Advertisements for Myself*) to be trying for that revelation through willful distortion which he achieved in *Barbary Shore*. One is curious to see the result.

I have gone into the chronology of Mailer's days and mine because they run parallel, occasionally crossing, and because the book he has just published is, in effect, an autobiography covering more or less his entire career with particular attention to the days of the Golfer's dull terror. Mailer gives us his life and his work together, and therefore it is impossible to review the book without attempting to make some estimate of both his character and the corpus of his work, the tension of his present and the shape of his future. Mailer is sly to get himself all this attention, but I must point out that it is a very dangerous move for an artist to expose himself so completely. Indeed, in other times it would have been fatal for an artist not yet full grown to show us his sores and wounds, his real and his illusory strength. Until very recently the artist was a magician who did his magic in public view but kept himself and his effects a matter of mystery. We know *now* of Flaubert's suffering, both emotional and aesthetic, during the days of his work, but it is hard to imagine what would have happened if the court which prosecuted *Madame Bovary* could have presented as evidence a volume of his letters. In effect, Mailer has anticipated his own posterity. He is giving us now the storms and the uncertainties, private and public, which he has undergone. He has armed the enemy and not entirely pleased his allies.

However, it may be possible to get away with this sort of thing today, for we live in the age of the confession. What Mailer has done is no different in kind from what those deranged and fallen actresses have accomplished in ghost-written memoirs where, with a shrewd eye on the comeback trail, they pathetically confess their sins to Demos, receiving for their tears the absolution of a culture obscenely interested in gossip. I suspect Mailer may create more interest in himself by having made this "clean breast of it" than he would have got by publishing a really distinguished novel. The audience no longer consumes novels, but it does devour personalities. Yet what happens after one is eaten? Is one regurgitated? Or does the audience move on to its next dinner of scandal and tears, its previous meal absorbed and forgotten?

Nevertheless, I am fairly certain that Mailer will survive everything. Despite a nice but small gift for self-destruction, he is uncommonly adroit, with an eye to the main chance (the writer who lacks this instinct is done for in America; excellence is not nearly enough). I

noted with some amusement that, despite his air of
candor, he makes no new enemies in this book. He
scores off those who are lost to him anyway, thus prov-
ing that essentially the work is politic. His confessions,
when not too disingenuous, are often engaging and
always interesting, as he tries to record his confusions.
For Mailer does not begin to know what he believes
or is or wants. His drive seems to be toward power of a
religio-political kind. He is a messiah without real hope
of paradise on earth or in heaven, and with no precise
mission except that dictated by his ever-changing temperament. I am not sure, finally, that he should be a
novelist at all, or even a writer, despite formidable
gifts. He is too much a demagogue; he swings from
one position of cant to another with an intensity that is
visceral rather than intellectual. He is all fragments and
pieces. He appears to be looking for an identity, and
often it seems that he believes crude celebrity will
give it to him again. The author of *The Naked and
the Dead*, though not the real Mailer, was at least an
identifiable surrogate, and duly celebrated. But Mailer
was quickly bored with the war-novelist role, and as
soon as possible he moved honorably to a new position:
radical politics, in the hope that through Marxist
action he might better identify himself to us and to himself. But that failed him, too. Nor is the new Mailer,
prophet of Hip and celebrator of sex and its connection
with time, apt to interest him or us for very long.

I also noted at moments toward the end of this book

that a reaction was setting in: Mailer started using military allusions. "Back in the Philippines, we . . ." —that sort of thing. And there were references to patrols, ambushes. It was startling. Most of our generation was in the war, usually ingloriously, yet I have never heard a contemporary make any reference to it in a personal way. The war to most of us was a profound irrelevance; traumatic for some, perhaps, but for most no more than an interruption. When the 1959 Mailer reminds us that he was a rifleman on Luzon, I get embarrassed for him and hope he is not going back to his first attitude to get the attention he wants.

Now for the book itself. It is a collection of stories, essays, notes, newspaper columns and part of a play. It begins with his first story at Harvard and ends with part of his new novel. The play, which I read in an earlier version, could be remarkable onstage. But the best work in this volume is two short stories. "The Language of Men" tells of the problems of an army cook who has an abstract passion for excellence as well as a need for the approbation of the indifferent men who eat his food. His war with them and himself and his will to excel are beautifully shown and in many ways make one of the best stories of its kind I have read, certainly preferable to Hemingway's *The Old Man and the Sea,* which it resembles in theme. But where Hemingway was pretentious and external, Mailer is particular and works with gentle grace from within his characters. The other story, "The Patron Saint of Macdougal Alley," is a wildly funny portrait of an archetypal drifter, and I think it is of permanent value: we have had this sort of fool in every age (Catullus and Juvenal each dealt with him), but I have not seen him done quite so well in our day.

By and large, excepting "The White Negro," I did not like the essays and the newspaper columns. Mailer is forever shouting at us that he is about to tell us something we must know or has just told us something revelatory and we failed to hear him or that he will, God grant his poor abused brain and body just one more chance, get through to us so that we will *know*. Actually, when he does approach a point he shifts into a swelling, throbbing rhetoric which is not easy to read but usually has something to do with love and sex and the horror of our age and the connection which must be made between time and sex (the image this bit of rhetoric suggests to me is a limitless gray sea of time with a human phallus desperately poking at a corner of it). He is at his best (who is not?) when discussing his own works and days. The piece about getting *The Deer Park* published is especially good, and depressing for what it reveals about our society. But, finally, in every line he writes, despite the bombast, there is uncertainty: Who am I? What do I want? What am I saying? He is Thomas Wolfe but with a conscience. Wolfe's motive for writing was perfectly clear: he wanted fame; he wanted to taste the whole earth, to name all the rivers. Mailer has the same passion for fame but he has a good deal more sense of responsibility and he sees that the thing is always in danger of spinning down into meaninglessness. Nothing is quite enough: art, sex, politics, drugs, God, mind. He is sure to get tired of Hip very soon. Sex will be a dead end for him, because sex is the one purely existential act. Sex is. There is nothing more to be done about it. Sex builds no roads, writes no novels, and sex certainly gives no meaning to anything in life but itself. I have often thought that much of D. H. Lawrence's self-lacerating hysteria toward the end of his life must have come out of some "blood knowledge" that the cruel priapic god was mad, bad and dangerous to know, and, finally, not even palliative to the universal strangeness.

Perhaps what has gone wrong in Mailer, and in many of our fellow clerks, is the sense that human beings to flourish must be possessed by one idea, a central meaning to which all experience can be related. To be, in Isaiah Berlin's bright metaphor, hedgehog rather than fox. Yet the human mind is not capable of this kind of exclusivity. We are none of us hedgehogs or foxes, but both simultaneously. The human mind is in continual flux, and personality is simply a sum of those attitudes which most often repeat themselves in recognizable actions. It is naïve and dangerous to try to impose on the human mind any system of thought which lays claim to finality. Very few first-rate writers have ever subordinated their own apprehension of a most protean reality to a man-made system of thought. Tolstoi's famous attempt in *War and Peace* nearly wrecked that beautiful work. Ultimately, not Christ, not Marx, not Freud, despite the pretensions of each, has the final word to say about the fact of being human. And those who take solemnly the words of other men as absolute are, in the deepest sense, maiming their own sensibilities and controverting the evidence of their own senses in a fashion which may be comforting to a terrified man but is disastrous for an artist.

One of the few sad results of the collapse of the Judeo-Christian ethical and religious systems has been the displacement of those who are absolutists by temperament and would in earlier times have been rabbis, priests, systematic philosophers. As the old Establishment of the West crumbles, the absolutists have turned to literature and the arts, and one by one the arts in the twentieth century have become hieratic. Serious literature has become religion, as Matthew Arnold foresaw. Those who once would have been fulfilled in Talmudic debate or suffered finely between the pull of Rome and the Church of England have turned to the writing of novels and, worse, to the criticism of novels. Now I am not sure that the novel, though it is many things, is particularly suited to didacticism. It is certainly putting an undesirable weight upon it to use it as a pretext for sermons or the resuscitation of antique religious myths. Works of fiction, at best, create not arguments but worlds, and a world by definition is an attitude toward a complex of experience, not a single argument or theme, syllogistically proposed. In the nineteenth century most of our critics (and many of our novelists) would have been writing books of sermons and quarreling over points of doctrine. With religion gone out of the intellectual world they now write solemnly and uneasily about novels; they are clearly impatient with the vulgar vitality of the better novels, and were it not that they had one another's books about books to analyze, I suspect many of them would despair and falter. The novelists don't seem very bright to the critics, while their commentaries seem irrelevant to the novelists. Yet each affects the other; and those writers who are unduly eager for fame and acceptance will write novels which they hope might interest "religious"-minded critics. The results range from the subliterary bleating of the Beats to Mailer's portentous cry which takes the form of: I am the way and the life ever after, crucify me, you hackers, for mine is a ritual death! Take my flesh and my blood, partake of me and *know* mysteries . . . ! And the curious thing is that they will crucify him; they will partake of his flesh; yet no mystery will be revealed. For the priests have created the gods, and they are all of them ritual harvest gods.

I was most struck by this remark of André Gide in the posthumous *Ainsi Soit-il:* "It is affectation that makes so many of today's writings, often even the best among them, unbearable to me. The author takes on a tone that is not natural to him." Of course it is sometimes the

work of a lifetime for an artist to discover who he is and
it is true that a great deal of good art results from the
trying on of masks, the affectation of a persona not
one's own. But it seems to me that most of my contemporaries, including Mailer, are — as Gide suggests —
desperately trying to convince themselves and the audience that they are something they are not. There is
even a certain embarrassment about writing novels at
all. Telling stories does seem a silly occupation for one
fully grown; yet to be a philosopher or a religious is not
easy when one is making a novel. Also, in a society such
as ours, where there is no moral, political or religious
center, the temptation to fill the void is irresistible.
There is the empty throne, so . . . *seize* the crown!
Who would not be a king or high priest in such an age?
And the writers, each in his own way, are preoccupied
with power. Some hope to achieve place through good
deportment. Universities are filled with poets and
novelists conducting demure and careful lives in
imitation of Eliot and Forster and those others who
(through what *seems* to have been discretion) made
it. Outside the universities one finds the buccaneers
who mean to seize the crown by force, blunt Boling-
brokes to the Academy's gentle Richards.

Mailer is a Bolingbroke, a born usurper. He will raise
an army anywhere, live off the country as best he can,
helped by a devoted underground, even assisted at
brief moments by rival claimants like myself. Yet when
all is said, none of this is the way to live. And it is not a

way (at least it makes the way harder) to create a
literature that, no doubt quixotically, remains the interest of each of us. I suppose if it helps Hemingway to
think of literature as a Golden Gloves Tournament with
himself pounding Maupassant to the mat or fighting
Stendhal to a draw, then no doubt the fantasy has
been of some use. But there is also evidence that the
preoccupation with power is a great waste of time.
Mailer has had the honesty to confess that his own competitiveness has wasted him as he worries about reviewers and bad publicity and the seemingly spiteful
successes of other novelists. Yet all the time he knows
perfectly well that writers are not in competition with
one another. The real enemy is the audience, which
grows more and more indifferent to literature, an audience which can be reached only by phenomena, by
superior pornographies or willfully meretricious accounts of the way we live now. No serious American
novelist has ever had any real sense of audience.
C. P. Snow made the point that he would, given a
choice, prefer to be a writer in England to a writer in
America because, for better or worse, the Establishment of his country would read him and know him as
he knew them, as the Greek dramatists knew and were
known by their city's audience. One cannot imagine the
American President, any American President, reading
a work by a serious contemporary American writer.
This lack of response is to me at the center of Mailer's
desperation. He is a public writer, not a private artist;

he wants to influence those who are alive at this time, but they will not notice him even when he is good. So each time he speaks he must become more bold, more loud, put on brighter motley and shake more foolish bells. *Anything* to get their attention, and finally (and this could be his tragedy) so much energy is spent in getting the indifferent ear to listen that when the time comes for him to speak there may be not enough strength or creative imagination left him to say what he *knows*. Exhausted, he becomes like Louis Lambert in Balzac's curious novel of the visionary-artist who, having seen straight through to the heart of the mystery, dies mad, murmuring: "The angels are white."

Yet of all my contemporaries I retain the greatest affection for Mailer as a force and as an artist. He is a man whose faults, though many, add to rather than subtract from the sum of his natural achievement. There is more virtue in his failures than in most small, premeditated successes which, in Cynic's phrase, "debase currency." Mailer, in all that he does, whether he does it well or ill, is honorable, and that is the highest praise I can give any writer in this piping time.*

[The *Nation*, January 2, 1960.]

---

* See Note 7 in the Appendix.

CARSON McCULLERS'S "CLOCK WITHOUT HANDS"

I T IS HARD to believe that twenty-one years have passed since *The Heart Is A Lonely Hunter,* the first novel of Carson McCullers, was published. For those of us who arrived on the scene in the war years, McCullers was *the* young writer. She was an American legend from the beginning, which is to say that her fame was as much the creation of publicity as of talent. The publicity was the work of those fashion magazines where a dish of black-eyed peas can be made to seem the roe of some rare fish, photographed by Avedon; yet McCullers's dreaming, androgynous face in its ikon elegance subtly confounded the chic of the lingerie ads all about her. For unlike other "legends," her talent was as real as her face. Though she was progenitress to much "Southern writing" (one can name a dozen writers who

178

would not exist in the way they do if she had not written in the way she did), she had a manner all her own. Her prose was chaste and severe, and realistic in its working out of narrative. I suspect that of all the Southern writers, she is the most apt to endure, though her vision is by no means as large or encompassing as that, say, of Faulkner, whom she has the grace to resemble not at all.

Southern writing — we have had such a lot of it in the last thirty years! Novelist after novelist has come to us out of the South, and there is no doubt that the Southern gift for the novel is as real as the Southern town, where family groups are more concentrated and less mobile than in the North. The Industrial Revolution was a long time coming South, and until recently the young Southerner was not apt to be thrown into the commercial world quite so soon or so fiercely as his Northern counterpart. But above all, there are the stories. Southerners talk and talk, tell and tell. In the rural areas, spinning long intricate stories of character is still a social skill. Up North, everyday conversation is mostly the repeating of the generalized anecdote: "You know the one about this man who met this woman who. . . ." In the South, it is: "When your cousin Hattie, she was Eula's stepsister, which makes her second cousin to James Edward, had to quit her job at the Court House after the fire, she met the Tutwiler boy, the one who tried to kill his father Memorial Day. . . ." They talk in chronicles and annals. They talk in novels.

It is not that life is more interesting in the South than elsewhere. Rather, it is the pleasure the people take in talking of neighbors and kin; the long memories and the delight in pondering that vast web of relationship which for three centuries has spun itself (white web!) over the red earth of what was wilderness.

From the beginning the South was provincial and middle-class. Its delusions of aristocracy began before the Civil War, when the novels of Sir Walter Scott took the plantation owners — and the not too many others who could read — by storm. Deliberately and disastrously, they modeled themselves on the folk of Scott's imagination. Faulkner's Sartoris is drawn not from fact but from Scott. Yet this lunatic dream of blue blood and inner grace is useful to an imaginative child. I doubt if there is a Southerner alive who has not been told in youth by at least one female relative, "Never forget *who* you are!" And yet who is this *who*? Just a plain middle-class child, usually of a lower-income group, with nothing grander in his family tree than a doctor or a lawyer or maybe an itinerant preacher. Yet to be told that you are, through blood, a Somebody starts a magic in the veins, starts dreams of empire and dominion, dreams of making, and, if the balance is right, in time the dream becomes reality and art *is* made.

The first thing to remark in McCullers is her style. From Wolfe to Faulkner, most Southern writing has tended to windy rhetoric of the "lost, lost and by the wind grieved" sort which I find entirely detestable. I can read very little of Wolfe, and much of the admirable Faulkner is ruined for me by that terrible gaseous prose (he went the length of *Requiem for a Nun* obsessively using "euphemistic" for "euphonious"). McCullers writes an exact prose closer to the Flaubert of *Un Cœur Simple* than to *Absalom, Absalom*. But her material is intensely Southern. Although she has had at times a passion for the extreme situation and the gratuitous act (*The Ballad of the Sad Café, Reflections in a Golden Eye*), whose intent I sometimes question, her means have always saved her. She gets entirely within the event told. There is never a false note. Technically, it is breathtaking to watch her set a scene and then dart from character to character, opening up in a line, a phrase, a life. It is marvelous, but . . .

But. Twenty-one years is a long time. *The Member of the Wedding*, her latest novel until now, was published in 1946. During those fifteen years other writers have come and gone. New attitudes, new follies, new perceptions have occurred to us. But most important, the world of the private vision which was her domain has been more and more intruded upon by the public world which threatens to destroy, literally, the actual world. Worse, though it may not do this final thing, the threat of extinction has made many doubt the worth of art. If the planet becomes an empty desert, why make anything, knowing it will soon be no more than a grain or two in the never-to-be-noticed dust? Not every writer of course has this apocalyptic vision, nor does a writer necessarily find the thought of the world's end any reason for not making what he wants to make in the present, which is all. But that ugly final thing *is* there, public and menacing and chilling the day. It is hard not to take it into account.

In her new novel, *Clock without Hands,* Carson McCullers acknowledges the public world for the first time in her work. Though her response is uneasy and uncertain, it is good to note that she writes as well as ever, with all the old clarity and fine tension. But the book is odd, and it is so because what has always been the most private of responses has been rudely startled and bemused by the world outside. The changing South. The Supreme Court Decision. Integration. The aviator as new man. All these things crop up unexpectedly in her narrative. One cannot say she handles these things badly; it is just that they do not quite fit her story of a gross old man (judge and white supremacist), his grandson (adolescent air voyager, perceptive), a dying druggist named Malone (who unexpectedly tries to stop a lynching), a colored youth (mad with hurt and self-delusion: is he really Marion Anderson's son left by her in a pew of a church in this Georgia town?). The four characters interact. They are explored. They come alive. Yet one is not convinced by the story told. Symbolically, is it true or merely pat?

At the book's end, the old judge, enraged by the Supreme Court's decision, goes on radio to denounce the

Court, but in his dottiness and great age he cannot recall anything to say except, word for word, the Gettysburg Address. Are we to take that as the South's last gasp as a new order begins? If so, I don't believe it. McCullers of course is free to make whatever she wants of a public situation. One quarrels not with her view of things, which is after all intuitive not liberal, but with the effect publicness has had on her art. Everything is thrown slightly out of kilter. She is not the only writer to suffer in this way. More and more of our private artists have fallen silent in the last twenty years, unable to cope with a world which has thrust itself upon the imagination like some clumsy-hooved animal loose in a garden. But even this near failure of McCullers is marvelous to read, and her genius for prose remains one of the few satisfying achievements of our second-rate culture.

[The *Reporter*, September 28, 1961.]

IN THE SHADOW OF THE SCALES: FRIEDRICH DUERRENMATT

LOVE, LIKE A SENSE of humor, is now claimed by everyone even though Love, like a sense of humor, is rather more rare than not, and to most of us poor muddlers unbearable at full strength. Our literature both popular and serious is drenched with Love, possessed by Love, usually sexual, though *caritas* will do; and if one only had a dollar for every time the word "compassion" has been used to describe some writer's best quality, one would be rich indeed. In the theater, where contemporary prejudices and superstitions are traditionally revealed at their most naked, Love has become *deus ex machina*. Our age has chosen its device (Eros crossed by the male and female biological symbols) and, in America at least, all other themes have been forsaken, dashed to bits on Dover Beach.

184

But now, like an avalanche in far-off mountains, comes Friedrich Duerrenmatt, a Swiss detective-story writer with a gift for the theater, to give us a new theme, or rather to remind us of an ancient one: justice. And he has arraigned with wit our Loving time before that tribunal.

I have read three of Duerrenmatt's eight novels, two of his six plays. I have studied his photograph on dust jackets — an interesting and not entirely irrelevant sport: the way a man chooses to be photographed is always significant. Duerrenmatt is thirty-seven and looks older. He is disarmingly fat (in each novel we get at least one rich dinner, ecstatically described). Yet he poses with a cold eye and a set mouth. His posture (to use a word beloved by the Golfer whom Heaven has put over us) is that of a judge, a hanging judge. As for his career, he has been writing since 1947 and his novels all seem to be thrillers, moral melodramas, while his plays include a Broadway success, *The Visit,* and the brilliant *Fools Are Passing Through,* which failed off-Broadway.

I realize my characterization of Duerrenmatt's novels will have created a certain unease: if they are really only thrillers, why bother with them? And at first glance, it is odd that Duerrenmatt, a moralist of the first rank who could so easily write "serious" novels about Love, should have chosen the detective novel as the form best suited for his particular vision. Duerrenmatt's own explanation is somewhat startling. In a recent essay, he comments on our time's stultifying literary climate, where writing is "studied but not made" and where "the demands made on the artist by aesthetics increase from day to day." Wanting to create but not wanting to do it in the manner fashionable, he proposes with engaging candor that "Perhaps the writer can best exist by writing detective stories, by creating art where it is least suspected. Literature must become so light that it will weigh nothing upon the scale of today's literary criticism; only in this way will it regain its true worth." A paradox calculated to chill the classrooms of the academy.

Yet assuming that we know what is meant by art in the novel (*the exercise of an unusual sensibility in order to illuminate the human prospect* . . . all right?), has Duerrenmatt on his own terms made art in the novel? Of the three books I have read in translation (*The Pledge, Traps, The Judge and the Hangman*), I would say that in the first two he has, although I find his chosen manner limiting. Where he is free and inventive in the theater, he is formal and conventional in the novel: the perverse opposite of most dramatist-novelists who tend to construct plays like clocks and improvise novels like Comus's rout. But these books are fascinating as expressions of a perverse and cranky mind obsessed with the idea of justice; and if they are less effective, less brilliant than his plays, I suspect it is because he has chosen to beguile the simpler reader, to evade the higher criticism, to impart lightly a serious vision.

Duerrenmatt's novels follow the classic mystery-story line: a crime is committed, the criminal is discovered, justice is done. Duerrenmatt's crimes are usually murder; the detection is precise; only in the ultimate justice does he transcend his form. It is here the comic ironist reveals himself. In *Traps,* the best of the novels, a traveling salesman's car breaks down. An elderly man, a former judge, puts him up for the night. There is a dinner party. The guests are a former prosecutor, a former defense attorney and a former executioner. During one of Duerrenmatt's better dinners (six lavish courses), they play a game. The salesman, a very ordinary opportunist, is put on trial for the murder of his predecessor in the firm. The predecessor died of a heart attack, but actually the salesman could have been — indeed was, as the trial progresses — morally responsible. The old men are devotees of crime, for it is "crime alone which makes justice possible." In a mad drunken scene, they convince the salesman that "he had killed because it was only natural for him to squeeze somebody else out," and they sentence him to death — a sentence he finds eminently just. Then, as final turn to the screw, though Duerrenmatt has prepared us for the salesman's execution at the hands of the old men, the salesman hangs himself in expiation, much to the surprise of the old men.

In *The Pledge* a little girl is found murdered. (It seems like only yesterday that Shirley Temple sang "On the Good Ship *Lollypop*"; how dangerous times have become for the small girl!) Matthäi, a soon-to-be-retired police inspector, promises the child's mother that he will bring the murderer to justice. A peddler is arrested; he commits suicide; the case is closed. But Matthäi, knowing the peddler was innocent, and himself mad with justice, devotes what turns out to be the rest of his life to finding the true murderer. Years pass. Matthäi waits patiently. He prepares an ingenious trap. The murderer almost falls into it, but at the last moment he evades Matthäi's justice. Matthäi continues to wait but his prey eludes him to the end. By accident the narrator, another policeman, discovers the murderer's identity. It is an irony within an irony.

Duerrenmatt has chosen his seedy protagonists with deliberate care, since, in his own words, "The state today cannot be envisioned, for it is anonymous and bureaucratic. . . . Any small-time crook, petty government official or policeman better represents our world than a senator or president. Today art can only embrace the victims, if it can reach men at all; it can no longer come close to the mighty. Creon's secretaries close Antigone's case."

The victims are Duerrenmatt heroes, for they must struggle in a society grown vast and impersonal. But though to Duerrenmatt "the universal is chaos," and though he has rejected superstition and dogma (*Fools*

Are Passing Through is a satire on true believers, the "100-per-centers," as he calls them), he does not reject the idea of justice, of law. Put paradoxically, he says: There is no divine law but we disobey it at our peril. Put simply: We are responsible for our acts even though there is no God. If man is to survive in a non-human universe of which he is a trifling part, the idea of justice must be maintained, for without justice there is chaos, as Duerrenmatt shows most plainly in *The Visit,* whose furious ending is *The Eumenides* in reverse.

Friedrich Duerrenmatt's vision is a cold one but pure, and very nearly unique in our day, for in his devotion to the idea of justice he has succeeded in casting across an age committed to false Love the dark shadow of the scales.

[The *Reporter,* April 30, 1959.]

BOOK REPORT: ROBERT PENN WARREN'S "BAND OF ANGELS"

Cᴀɴ ʏᴏᴜ ʜᴇᴀʀ ᴍᴇ? Oh, good. Then I won't have to use this thing. It scares me to death! My husband always tells me, "Marian, you and your mother may not be very good but you're certainly loud enough when you give a book report." That's what he always says. Now then: the book I'm going to talk to you about today is by an American writer named Robert Penn Warren. Robert Penn Warren. He has written some poems, and of course most of us read his book a few years ago called *All the King's Men,* which they later made a movie out of and ruined, the way they always do. Mr. Warren's new book is a historical — *an* historical — novel *with a difference.* It begins with a beautiful quotation from a poem by A. E. Housman, the poet:

"When shall I be dead and rid of the wrong my father did?"

And that's just what it's about. About Amantha Starr, a beautiful girl of sixteen, raised in Ohio where she'd been sent to be educated by her father — sent by her father to be educated — a wealthy Kentucky plantation owner. When suddenly he dies, she comes home for his funeral, where she finds that not only did he die bankrupt, but that she is really a Negress, the daughter of one of his slaves, and she has to be sold to pay off these debts he left. Well, this is how the story starts. A really awful situation for a girl to be in. One day she had everything money and refinement could bring, and the next day she is a slave. The very first sentence of the book is filled with symbolism: "Oh, who am I? For so long that was, you might say, the cry of my heart." And then there follows a description of this wonderful house she lived in in Kentucky, south of Lexington, near Danville: a two-story brick house with a chimney at each end and a portico with pillars. The most beautiful house you could imagine! All of which she lost when she found she was colored and sold to a dealer who took her to New Orleans where she was put up for sale in the slave market as a slave.

Fortunately, she was bought by the most interesting person in the book, a fascinating older man with a lame leg who always walked with a heavy blackthorn stick with a great silver knob. His name was Hamish Bond, and he became her protector. Not until much later does she find out that he's really not named Bond but Hinks, that he was raised in Baltimore where he was a slave trader, going to Africa regularly and bringing back Negroes. He had some awful experiences in Africa. One in particular, a description of a massacre, is really gruesome where these Amazon women go through an entire village, slaughtering all the men, women and children because they're so enormous and bloodthirsty, much stronger than men. When Hamish, whose real name is Hinks, tries to keep one of the Amazons from killing a baby, this is what happens: "I just shoved her a little. It's very peculiar the way you have a habit. I just shoved her gentle because she was, in a way of speaking, a lady, and I had learned manners back in Baltimore. Here she was a crocodile-hided, blood-drinking old frau, who had been in her line of business for twenty years, and I caught myself making allowance for a lady." Well, he wished he hadn't, because right after he pushed her she slashed his leg with a big razor, making a long jagged cut which is what made him lame and why he had to always walk with that blackthorn cane with the silver knob.

Anyway, Hamish was kind in his brooding way to Amantha, and he treated her like she was really a lady which made her feel a bit better about being a slave. As somebody in the book says, the trouble with Hamish is he has "kindness like a disease." Another fascinating character Amantha meets is Hamish's *k'la* (meaning Negro best friend) Rau-ru, "whose eyes were wide, large and deepset, his nose wide but not flattened, the underlip full if not to the comic fullness favored in the minstrel shows of our day, and the corners of the mouth were drawn back so that the effect of that mouth was one of arrogant reserve and not blubbering docility."

Hamish was a very unusual man, especially after the Civil War started. One night there is a storm at Hamish's house — and Hamish takes Amantha in his arms while the rain blows in the window and she knows for the first time what love is. "With the hand of Hamish Bond laid to my side, and the spreading creep and prickle of sensation across the softness of my belly from the focus of Hamish Bond's sandpaper thumb, and the unplaiting and deliquescence of the deep muscles of thighs were as much History as any death-cry at the trenchlip or in the tangle of the abatis."

Can you still hear me? Well, that's how she feels as she discovers what love is and this maybe is the only serious fault in the book. I mean *would* a young girl like Amantha, even though she was well educated in Oberlin, Ohio, think thoughts quite like *that*? I mean, older more experienced women would, but would she? However, Mr. Warren writes poetic English and we can certainly excuse an occasional symbolic sentence like that. Well, there are many beautiful passages like this in the book, but the story never gets bogged down and the parts about the Civil War are really fascinating. Especially in New Orleans where she meets, completely by accident, Seth Parton, her girlhood sweetheart, who is now an officer in the Union Army, and also Tobias Sears, "the New England idealist to whom the butcheries of war must be justified by 'truth.'" I don't think it will spoil the book any if I tell you that everything ends all right with Tobias and Amantha . . . Miss Manty, as everybody calls her . . . together in quite a beautiful and touching ending.

I'd like to say something, by the way, if I may make a digression, about the much-maligned historical novel . . . the "bosom books" as they are disdainfully called by some critics, who think they know everything and can't keep from tearing apart books like Mr. Warren's. Now, I know and you know that maybe these books aren't *exactly* history, but they're awfully close, some of them, especially this one, and I can't help but think of Mrs. Gregg Henderson's fascinating report some meetings ago about the boys in Korea who were captured and tortured and brainwashed by the Chinese Communists who found that American boys were easy to break down BECAUSE THEY DID NOT KNOW ENOUGH ABOUT AMERICAN HISTORY AND WHY THEY WERE FIGHTING. Most of us here are mothers and we all know the trouble we have getting boys to read about history and all the things which don't seem important to them until they're caught by the enemy, when it's too late. So I don't think it's fair to make fun of novels that may be a little romantic but are still very useful ways of teaching what America is to people who are never going to read history or really deep things. I think Mr. Warren has done a wonderful job of bringing to life the Civil War and certain problems of that time — and frankly, I don't care a penny what the critics say about the book. After all, if people didn't want books like this, writers wouldn't write them and publishers wouldn't publish them. You can't argue with facts!

This book has been high on the best-seller list, and the movies have bought it, though they'll probably ruin it like they always do. A lot of people are going to be hearing about Amantha Starr and the Civil War. And they'll learn something. I firmly believe that these characters will stay with you for many a long day. Rau-ru, Miss Manty, the Amazons who go into that village killing all the men, Hamish Bond with his heavy blackthorn stick with the great silver knob — all these wonderful characters come alive for you in the pages of *Band of Angels* by Robert Penn Warren, published by Random House, three hundred and seventy-five pages long. Long? I wanted it to go on forever, and so will you!

[*Zero,* Spring 1956.]

THE MAKING OF A HERO
AND A LEGEND: RICHARD HILLARY

LOVAT DICKSON was Richard Hillary's English publisher and this book is an affectionate if cursory biography of Hillary as well as an illuminating footnote to that remarkable work which was published in England nine years ago as *The Last Enemy* and in America as *Falling Through Space*.

Richard Hillary was born in Australia, the only child of civil servants who sent him to the proper public schools in England, where he grew to be a handsome, athletic, scornful, clever youth: in his own words "an alert Philistine." With a group of friends from Oxford ("the long-haired boys") he joined the R.A.F. in 1939 as a fighter pilot. He flew against the Germans until, having survived all his comrades, he himself was shot down, his face and hands badly burned.

After nightmare months in various hospitals, he emerged at last with a new face, a patchwork of skin grafts, and clawlike hands with which, painfully, he composed *The Last Enemy*, a description of that ordeal which had changed him from a rather nihilistic Oxford undergraduate to a man who had, through pain, experienced a sense of the world's community.

Yet the hero seldom remains one with humanity: rather humanity becomes one with the hero, absorbed in the high gallantry of his legend. It became one with Hillary when, the book finished, he, sick and frightened, went back on active duty against the orders of his doctors and was killed, as he knew that he would be.

Arthur Koestler in "The Birth of Myth" (*Horizon*, April 1943) attempted with passion and ingenuity to define not only Hillary's sacrifice but his equivocal attitude toward the meaning of war, toward courage and responsibility, recording, as does Mr. Dickson, his dislike of the resonant clichés of politicians and his inarticulate obsession with virtue. He suffered, Koestler finally decided, from what French Catholics call *la maladie du scrupule*.

Mr. Dickson, however, keeps to the periphery of his hero's life, collecting with care the relevant letters, the anecdotes the living had to tell. The central mystery being left for the reader to determine as he pleases. Even Hillary himself never quite understood the reason for his last gesture. He could only suggest that it was instinct rather than vanity which guided him, and that he did believe, finally, that the war was to be the beginning of something better in the world, never realizing that his act in itself *was* that something better men awaited, a bright moment whose memory would endure long after the war's urgency had become a schoolboy's dreary lesson.

Hillary belongs to that small company of the Western world's writers who have written with poetic as well as literal truth of war: Crane, St.-Exupéry — there have been few in our day. Among those few, Hillary is unique, for he died a legend in a time when heroism was unpopular. Like his generation, he had no faith, served no dogma, mocked always the jargon of chivalry while, paradoxically, demonstrating an antique virtue which was indeed remarkable when one considers not only the era in which he lived but the fact that when he died he was just twenty-three.

[*New York Times Book Review*, February 11, 1951.]

FOOTNOTE TO THE DREYFUS CASE

In october, 1894, the young Maurice Paléologue, ambassador and Academician-to-be, was assigned by the French Foreign Office to act as special liaison between the Quai d'Orsay and that curious moral melodrama, *l'affaire Dreyfus*. As the scandal unfolded in all its puzzling intricacy, Paléologue kept a journal that, published now for the first time as *An Intimate Journal of the Dreyfus Case*, captures as perhaps no other account does the day-by-day tension of a five-year crisis that was to split the political and the social life of France, leaving scars to this day unhealed.

Captain Alfred Dreyfus was an ordinary, rather unappealing man whose only distinction before his tragic case was his appointment to the general staff. He was the first Jew ever to be accepted in the inner circle of an army that was traditionally anti-Semitic, romantically tracing its descent from those lively opportunists, the Crusaders of the Middle Ages.

The appointment of Dreyfus was an experiment in liberalism. Needless to say, it was resented by many officers, among them Colonel Sandherr, the splendidly egregious chief of counterintelligence, who resolutely maintained that Jewish racial loyalties could never coincide with French interests. But Sandherr was overruled, and Dreyfus was accepted as a probationer in January of 1893.

In the fall of 1894, an agent of counterintelligence stole from the German Embassy a memorandum, the famous *bordereau*, listing a number of secret and semisecret French military documents for sale. Moving rapidly and with stern illogic, Sandherr and his assistant, Major Henry, decided that Dreyfus was the spy. His handwriting, the fantastic M. Bertillon of the Sûreté declared, was the same as that of the *bordereau*. Later, when the defense revealed obvious dissimilarities Bertillon confidently maintained that Dreyfus had of course tried to disguise his writing. At subsequent trials, when the handwriting of Ferdinand Esterhazy, the actual spy, was found to be identical with that of the *bordereau*, the army blandly proposed that Dreyfus had deliberately imitated Esterhazy's hand. This sort of somber lunacy was to mark the entire affair.

Through Paléologue's eyes we observe the various stages of the crisis: The leak to the newspapers that forced the army to court-martial Dreyfus on no more

evidence than the *bordereau* and a false accusation
by Major Henry. The exile to Devil's Island. The efforts
of Dreyfus's brother and wife to reopen the case. The
apprehension of Esterhazy as the real spy. The army's
crude exoneration of Esterhazy. The ugly hysteria of
anti-Semitism. The rallying of French intellectuals to
Dreyfus's defense. The exhibitionistic but useful attack on the government by Zola; his subsequent trial
and conviction. The political and emotional alienation
of the intellectuals (and where will *that* end?) from
the bourgeois life of the nation. Major Henry's forged
evidence against Dreyfus; Henry's arrest and suicide.
Everything is recorded with dry clarity in Paléologue's
journal.

And there are revelations, too. Esterhazy, that remarkable melodramatist, was not the only spy. There
was another, whom Paléologue does not name, a high-
ranking officer "now commanding troops." There is also
a brilliant portrait of the clever, temperamental
President Casimir-Périer, whose dislike of the War
Minister, General Mercier (a marvelous figure beautifully preserved not here but in the amber of Proust's
Jean Santeuil), contributed so much to the final trial in
'99 when Dreyfus, again found guilty, was pardoned
and finally restored to his rank. One learns, too, in a
fresh way, what one has always suspected: that certain
high-ranking generals like Gonse were simply stupid
and that Dreyfus had bad luck in his lawyers. The first,
Demange, lacked energy, while the second, Labori, was

a demagogue whose thundering manner hopelessly antagonized the court. One is also grateful to find that at least Paléologue and the Foreign Office were aware from the beginning of the spuriousness of certain letters forged by Major Henry purporting to be from the Kaiser to Dreyfus; the fact they were ever thought authentic betrays a startling naïveté on the part of those military men and journalists who took for granted that emperors correspond intimately with minor secret agents.

This journal is certainly the most interesting record published so far of the Dreyfus case. It unfolds like a classic mystery novel, the reader knowing no more at any given moment than the narrator; almost an ideal form in which to render legal complexities. Yet for all of Paléologue's clarity, one has at times the uneasy impression that he is disingenuous. He confesses right off that he destroyed the original manuscript from which this narrative was taken. He also admits to certain rearrangements of the text, in the interest, he declares, of verisimilitude.

But Paléologue was an artist as well as a diplomatist, and one must allow him a certain license in his evocation of the past. His attitude, in any case, was civilized, and it is his posthumous gift to the world to remind the living once again of the profound significance of this melodrama. He poses the issue clearly: Does any institution, whether it be the general staff of an army or the governing arm of the body politic itself, have the right, for its own convenience, to sacrifice a man without regard for his innocence or guilt? It is especially useful now to be reminded of the way another age met and failed to resolve a perennial issue. Semantically, the case is interesting; because of it, a new word was coined: "intellectual," to describe those artists and scholars who, in sudden articulate congress, wanted justice done.*

[The *Reporter*, April 4, 1957.]

* See Note 8 in the Appendix.

ROBERT GRAVES AND
THE TWELVE CAESARS

T IBERIUS, Capri. Pool of water. Small children . . . So far so good. One's laborious translation was making awful sense. Then . . . Fish. Fish? The erotic mental image became surreal. Another victory for the Loeb Library's sly translator, J. C. Rolfe, who, correctly anticipating the pruriency of schoolboy readers, left Suetonius's gaudier passages in the hard original. One failed to crack those intriguing footnotes not because the syntax was so difficult (though it was not easy for students drilled in military rather than civilian Latin) but because the range of vice revealed was considerably beyond the imagination of even the most depraved schoolboy. There was a point at which one rejected one's own translation. Tiberius and the little fish, for instance.

Happily, we now have a full translation of the text, the work of Mr. Robert Graves, who, under the spell of his Triple Goddess, has lately been retranslating the classics. One of his first tributes to her was a fine rendering of *The Golden Ass;* then Lucan's *Pharsalia;* then the *Greek Myths,* a collation aimed at rearranging the hierarchy of Olympus to afford his Goddess (the female principle) a central position at the expense of the male. (Beware Apollo's wrath, Graves: the "godling" is more than front man for the "Ninefold Muse-Goddess.") Now, as a diversion, Mr. Graves has given us *The Twelve Caesars* of Suetonius in a good, dry, no-nonsense style; and, pleasantly enough, the Ancient Mother of Us All is remarkable only by her absence, perhaps a subtle criticism of an intensely masculine period in history.

Gaius Suetonius Tranquillus — lawyer and author of a dozen books, among them *Lives of Famous Whores* and *The Physical Defects of Mankind* (What was that about?) — worked for a time as private secretary to the Emperor Hadrian. Presumably it was during this period that he had access to the imperial archives, where he got the material for *The Twelve Caesars,* the only complete book of his to survive. Suetonius was born in A.D. 69, the year of the three Caesars Galba, Otho, Vitellius; and he grew up under the Flavians: Vespasian, Titus, Domitian, whom he deals with as contemporaries. He was also close enough in time to the first six Caesars to have known men who knew them intimately, at least from Tiberius on, and it is this place in time which gives such immediacy to his history.

Suetonius saw the world's history from 49 B.C. to A.D. 96 as the intimate narrative of twelve men wielding absolute power. With impressive curiosity he tracked down anecdotes, recording them dispassionately, despite a somewhat stylized reactionary bias. Like his fellow historians from Livy to the stuffy but interesting Dion Cassius, Suetonius was a political reactionary to whom the old Republic was the time of virtue and the Empire, implicitly, was not. But it is not for his political convictions that we read Suetonius. Rather, it is his gift for telling us what we want to know. I am delighted to read that Augustus was under five feet seven, blond, wore lifts in his sandals to appear taller, had seven birthmarks and weak eyes; that he softened the hairs of his legs with hot walnut shells, and liked to gamble. Or to learn that the droll Vespasian's last words were: "Dear me, I must be turning into a god." ("Dear me" being Graves for *"Vae."*) The stories, true or not, are entertaining, and when they deal with sex startling, even to a post-Kinseyan.

Gibbon, in his stately way, mourned that of the twelve Caesars only Claudius was sexually "regular." From the sexual opportunism of Julius Caesar to the sadism of Nero to the doddering pederasty of Galba, the sexual lives of the Caesars encompassed every aspect of what our post-medieval time has termed "sexual abnormality." It would be wrong, however, to dismiss, as so many commentators have, the wide variety of Caesarean

sensuality as simply the viciousness of twelve abnormal
men. They were, after all, a fairly representative lot.
They differed from us — and their contemporaries —
only in the fact of power, which made it possible for
each to act out his most recondite sexual fantasies.
This is the psychological fascination of Suetonius. What
will men so placed do? The answer, apparently, is anything and everything. Alfred Whitehead once remarked that one got the essence of a culture not by
those things which were said at the time but by those
things which were *not* said, the underlying assumptions
of the society, too obvious to be stated. Now it is an underlying assumption of twentieth-century America that
human beings are either heterosexual or, through some
arresting of normal psychic growth, homosexual, with
very little traffic back and forth. To us, the norm is
heterosexual; the family is central; all else is devia-
tion, pleasing or not depending on one's own tastes
and moral preoccupations. Suetonius reveals a very
different world. His underlying assumption is that man
is bisexual and that given complete freedom to love
— or, perhaps more to the point in the case of the
Caesars, to violate — others, he will do so, going
blithely from male to female as fancy dictates. Nor is
Suetonius alone in this assumption of man's variousness.
From Plato to the rise of Pauline Christianity, which tried
to put the lid on sex, it is explicit in classical writing.
Yet to this day Christian, Freudian and Marxian commentators have all decreed or ignored this fact of nature

in the interest each of a patented approach to the Kingdom of Heaven. It is an odd experience for a contemporary to read of Nero's simultaneous passion for both a man and a woman. Something seems wrong. It must be one or the other, not both. And yet this sexual eclecticism recurs again and again. And though some of the Caesars quite obviously preferred women to men (Augustus had a particular penchant for Nabokovian nymphets), their sexual crisscrossing is extraordinary in its lack of pattern. And one suspects that despite the stern moral legislation of our own time human beings are no different. If nothing else, Dr. Kinsey revealed in his dogged, arithmetical way that we are all a good deal less predictable and bland than anyone had suspected.

One of the few engaging aspects of the Julio-Claudians was authorship. They all wrote; some wrote well. Julius Caesar, in addition to his account of that famed crusade in Gaul, wrote an *Oedipus*. Augustus wrote an *Ajax*, with some difficulty. When asked by a friend what his *Ajax* had been up to lately, Augustus sighed: "He has fallen not on his sword, but wiped himself out on my sponge." Tiberius wrote an *Elegy on the Death of Julius Caesar*. The scatterbrained Claudius, a charmingly dim prince, was a devoted pedant who tried to reform the alphabet. He was also among the first to have a serious go at Etruscan history. Nero of course is remembered as a poet. Julius Caesar and Augustus were distinguished prose writers; each preferred plain old-fashioned Latin. Augustus particularly disliked what he called the "Asiatic" style, favored by, among others, his rival Marc Antony, whose speeches he found imprecise and "stinking of farfetched phrases."

Other than the fact of power, the twelve Caesars as men had little in common with one another. But that little was significant: a fear of the knife in the dark. Of the twelve, eight (perhaps nine) were murdered. As Domitian remarked not long before he himself was struck down: "Emperors are necessarily wretched men since only their assassination can convince the public that the conspiracies against their lives are real." In an understandable attempt to outguess destiny, they studied omens, cast horoscopes, and analyzed dreams (they were ingenious symbolists, anticipating Dr. Freud, himself a Roman buff). The view of life from Palatine Hill was not comforting, and though none of the Caesars was religious in our sense of the word, all inclined to the Stoic. It was Tiberius, with characteristic bleakness, who underscored their dangerous estate when he declared that it was Fate, not the gods, which ordered the lives of men.

Yet what, finally, was the effect of absolute power on twelve representative men? Suetonius makes it quite plain: disastrous. Caligula was certifiably mad. Nero, who started well, became progressively irrational. Even the stern Tiberius's character weakened. In fact,

Tacitus, in covering the same period as Suetonius, observes: "Even after his enormous experience of public affairs, Tiberius was ruined and transformed by the violent influence of absolute power." Caligula gave the game away when he told a critic, "Bear in mind that I can treat anyone exactly as I please." And that cruelty which is innate in human beings, now given the opportunity to use others as toys, flowered monstrously in the Caesars. Suetonius's case history (and it is precisely that) of Domitian is particularly fascinating. An intelligent man of some charm, trained to govern, Domitian when he first succeeded to the Principate contented himself with tearing the wings off flies, an infantile pastime which gradually palled until, inevitably, for flies he substituted men. His favorite game was to talk gently of mercy to a nervous victim; then, once all fears had been allayed, execute him. Nor were the Caesars entirely unobjective about their bizarre position. There is an oddly revealing letter of Tiberius to a Senate which had offered to ensure in advance approbation of all his future deeds. Tiberius declined the offer: "So long as my wits do not fail me, you can count on the consistency of my behavior; but I should not like you to set the precedent of binding yourselves to approve a man's every action; for what if something happened to alter that man's character?" In terror of their lives, haunted by dreams and omens, giddy with dominion, it is no wonder that actual insanity was often the Caesarean refuge from a reality so intoxicating.

The unifying *Leitmotiv* in these lives is Alexander the Great. The Caesars were fascinated by him. He was their touchstone of greatness. The young Julius Caesar sighed enviously at his tomb. Augustus had the tomb opened and stared long at the conqueror's face. Caligula stole the breastplate from the corpse and wore it. Nero called his guard the "Phalanx of Alexander the Great." And the significance of this fascination? Power for the sake of power. Conquest for the sake of conquest. Earthly dominion as an end in itself: no Utopian vision, no dissembling, no hypocrisy. I knock you down; now *I* am king of the castle. Why should young Julius Caesar be envious of Alexander? It does not occur to Suetonius to explain. He assumes that *any* young man would like to conquer the world. And why did Julius Caesar, a man of first-rate mind, want the world? Simply, to have it. Even the resulting Pax Romana was not a calculated policy but a fortunate accident. Caesar and Augustus, the makers of the Principate, represent the naked will to power for its own sake. And though our own society has not much changed from the Roman (we may point with somber pride to Hitler and Stalin, who lent a real Neronian hell to our days), we have, nevertheless, got so into the habit of dissembling motives, of denying certain dark constants of human behavior, that it is difficult to find a reputable American

historian who will acknowledge the crude fact that a
Franklin Roosevelt, say, wanted to be President merely
to wield power, to be famed and to be feared. To learn
this simple fact one must wade through a sea of eva-
sions: history as sociology, leaders as teachers, bland
benevolence as a motive force, when, finally, power *is*
an end to itself, and the instinctive urge to prevail the
most important single human trait, the necessary force
without which no city was built, no city destroyed. Yet
many contemporary sociologists and religionists turned
historians will propose, quite seriously: If there had not
been a Julius Caesar then the *Zeitgeist* would have
provided another like him, even though it is quite
evident that had this particular Caesar not existed no
one would have dared invent him. World events are
the work of individuals whose motives are often frivolous, even casual. Had Claudius not wanted an easy
conquest so that he might celebrate a triumph at Rome,
Britain would not have been conquered in A.D. 44. If
Britain had not been colonized in the first century . . .
the chain of causality is plain.

One understands of course why the role of the individual in history is instinctively played down by a
would-be egalitarian society. We are, quite naturally,
afraid of being victimized by reckless adventurers. To
avoid this we have created the myth of the ineluctable
mass ("other-directedness") which governs all. Science,

we are told, is not a matter of individual inquiry but of collective effort. Even the surface storminess of our elections disguises a fundamental indifference to human personality: if not this man, then that one; it's all the same; life will go on. Up to a point there is some virtue in this; and though none can deny that there is a prevailing grayness in our placid land, it is certainly better to be non-ruled by mediocrities than enslaved by Caesars. But to deny the dark nature of human personality is not only fatuous but dangerous. For in our insistence on the surrender of private will ("inner-directedness") to a conception of the human race as some teeming bacteria in the stream of time, unaffected by individual deeds, we have been made vulnerable not only to boredom, to that sense of meaninglessness which more than anything else is characteristic of our age, but vulnerable to the first messiah who offers the young and bored some splendid prospect, some Caesarean certainty. That is the political danger, and it is a real one.

Most of the world today is governed by Caesars. Men are more and more treated as things. Torture is ubiquitous. And, as Sartre wrote in his preface to Henri Alleg's chilling book about Algeria, "Anybody, at any time, may equally find himself victim or executioner." Suetonius, in holding up a mirror to those Caesars of diverting legend, reflects not only them but ourselves:

half-tamed creatures, whose great moral task it is to hold in balance the angel and the monster within — for we are both, and to ignore this duality is to invite disaster.

[1959.]

SOCIAL CLIMBING,
ACCORDING TO THE BOOKS

"How lucky you Americans are to have no class system!" All right. How do *you* answer that? The speaker is often English, and his tone is either wistful, if he is red-brick (lower middle-class), or gently malicious, if he is grey-stone (Establishment). My usual comment is a long, neutral "Well . . ." Not only have I never found a way of explaining our class system to a European, I have yet to find a satisfactory way of explaining it to myself. If pressed, I will admit that, although it is possible to live a successful life in the United States without ever noticing class differences, for those so minded our social structure is actually every bit as complex and hierarchic as the ancient Byzantine court, and equally frustrating for those who would master the maze of precedence. Precedence? In a democracy? "Inequality," observed William Dean Howells somewhat unexpectedly, "is as dear to the American heart as liberty itself."

Lately there have been a number of books dealing with American society, and now, since social advancement has become, in the glum phrase of one of the writers, a "status symbol," I suggest we take a cold look at the snobs about us and examine the art of the social climber, his tricks and devices, recalling with tolerance that grand old climber (transatlantic division) Henry James, who once remarked with a certain edge that the pursuit of a social career is as reasonable an aim in life as any other. Relevant to James, there is a fine story, I hope not apocryphal, of the American critic who was doing research on James in London. He met as many friends and acquaintances of James's as he could. Being American and academic, not used to the great world, he was thrilled by the Master's rich social life at the pinnacle of the beautifully intricate world of Edwardian London. The critic came finally to the grandest acquaintance of all, a lady who recalled Henry James amiably (though she preferred the books of Maurice Hewlett). When the professor commented on the rarefied social world in which James moved, the lady said quite firmly, "But don't you see? That's the whole point. Mr. James never knew the *right* people." The right people who dwell in the great good place — that is the Grail to the social climber, seldom, for reasons we shall explore, to be obtained in America.

The Private World of High Society is a wide-eyed account by Lucy Kavaler, a young woman whose love for her subject is genuine and touching. From the outside, she discusses what she thinks to be American "high society" in a manner meant to resemble, if not Margaret Mead, at least that of a pop-culture writer like Vance Packard. Actually, what she has come up with is a how-to-do-it book for lower-middle-class climbers who want to make a modest move up the ladder to the country club and the mass-debutante ball. In her how-to-do-it book, she has a number of useful tips. She shows how it is possible for a strong-willed woman with money to involve herself in a socially acceptable charity where she can meet those wheels of the community who are able to help her join the desirable clubs and launch her daughter socially, a matter of real urgency to ambitious middle-class parents. Miss Kavaler also has an informative chapter on the *Social Register* and on the inscrutable standards of its long-time arbitress, a train conductor's daughter named Mrs. Edwin C. Barry. She also set my mind at rest on one point. I was relieved to discover that there are fifty Meyer Davis bands, and that what I've thought for years was the most ubiquitous conductor of our time was often only a stand-in. Miss Kavaler discusses the "right" schools, observing sagely that for the second generation to move up the ladder attendance at one of the better prep schools is helpful. She also has some interesting things to say about the suburbs. In fact, she might have been wise to concentrate entirely on the recent phenomenal exodus from the cities to the surrounding countryside, and on the tensions caused by newcomers to old villages and to the once private enclaves of the rich. Many new suburbanites, she tells us, having failed to make it socially in New York, will move away, thinking it is simpler to get by in Scarsdale. Only, it is not simpler — and Miss Kavaler, with the compassion of a war correspondent surveying a bombed-out orphanage, records in detail the nervous breakdowns of ladies who failed to make the grade at the golf club, who met with unkindness at Gristede's, whose daughters were doomed never to hear the music of a Meyer Davis stand-in. It is poignant stuff.

Miss Kavaler is writing not about High Society but about the ever-enlarging, ever more affluent middle class. As people come from obscurity and low salaries to some degree of local recognition and increased income, there is a natural desire to be accepted by the visible Establishment of the community. Charity work, the right schools, disciplined conformity can get almost anyone from the lower middle class to the upper middle class in any city in the United States; but High Society (to use her phrase) is something quite different, which we'll get to in a moment.

Miss Kavaler also tends to fall into the error so many psychiatrists do: those who are willing to talk to her at length usually bear some wound, and she must build her case upon their evidence — just as psychiatrists often tend to generalize incorrectly from the distraught neurotics who necessarily make up their practice. *The World of High Society* is full of wonderfully naïve whoppers. Referring to Philadelphia, Miss Kavaler remarks with quiet authority: "It is one of the few remaining places where one can attend dinner parties and find the ladies retiring after the meal to leave the men to their brandy and cigars."

Cleveland Amory, on the other hand, knows exactly what he is writing about. He knows High Society and Café Society from the inside, and he has a number of good things to say about each. In his new book, *Who Killed Society?* (a bad title, because as long as people want to do things together that others would like to do but may not, there will be Society), Mr. Amory poses an interesting theorem. An American family on the rise goes through three phases: Celebrity, Society, Aristocracy. Some families get from the first phase to the second but not to the third. Few make all three stations of the ascent. The first step, Celebrity, is unarguable. By Celebrity, Mr. Amory means not only big money but national notice. Of course the qualifications for Celebrity have changed in our time. Today, anyone who can afford a press agent and has the endurance to be seen at night clubs and fashionable resorts can become, technically, a celebrity. But in earlier generations to be counted a celebrity one was either a big businessman, an Astor, a Vanderbilt, a Gould — men whose activities used to get as much press as movie stars do now — or else one was a man of state, an Adams, a Randolph, a Saltonstall.

I found Mr. Amory particularly interesting on the luck of families. Why did the Goulds not move from Society (which they had a hard time cracking at all, despite Celebrity) to Aristocracy, while the Belmonts touched all three bases with ease? Or why in every generation has the Adams family been extraordinary, not only intellectually but in the public interest, while a coeval family like the Schuylers vanished? Or by what fate, eugenic or environmental, have the Astors who went to England continued in the best aristocratic sense to be useful citizens while the American Astors are now represented solely by the much-married "Jackaster"?

Mr. Amory makes a strong but inconclusive case that the old High Society is dead and that only the current half-world of Celebrity holds the fort. First, there is the matter of money. Though Aristocracy can get along without big money, it cannot survive — at least in the larger, colder cities — without *some* money. Increased inheritance and income taxes have ended many dynasties. Second, there is the matter of servants. Traditionally, Society was based on a certain scale of living that is not possible without servants — a class now nearly extinct in America. One of Mr. Amory's sources remarks with some astuteness that the old order ended when people began to entertain one another in public restaurants and ballrooms. Aristocracy was never public. I once met an old lady who arrived at the same house and at the same time I arrived for dinner. As we went inside, she asked me quite seriously not to tell anyone I had seen her get out of a "public taxicab." You entertained at home; you traveled in your own car. The third item is publicity. If Aristocracy tries to compete with the modern Celebrity, Aristocracy usually comes off a poor second. Whenever Mr. Amory's characters (it is a tribute to his gifts that I keep thinking of his factual work as a vast novel) fall for the bright busy world of publicity, they are invariably outdone by the real publicity operators — and that is the end of them.

Mr. Amory defines the aristocrat as one who, though private in his personal life, has a strong sense of public obligation; he also tends to be remarkably candid in speech. Since the principal characteristic of the middle class in any country at any time is hypocrisy, aristocratic candor is as refreshing and sometimes as terrifying as the candor of the lowest class. It is often hair-raising. I know one American aristocrat of great age who still refers genially to the venerable Bernard Baruch as one of the better "Jew-boys." There is very little mincing of words at the top. Unfortunately, since we have never quite known what to do with our aristocrats, how to train and educate them, those unminced words are often fatuous. As a result, excepting those whose families for several generations have been dominated by stern patriarchs (Adamses, du Ponts, such new aristocrats as the Rockefellers), our aristocracy tends to deteriorate into fatheadedness.

Mr. Amory makes one observation that I found fascinating, and I wish he had gone into it more thoroughly: Until the 1920's there was very little anti-Semitism in our society. The Jewish-American aristocracy (Strauses, Warburgs, Lehmans, and so on), which goes back to 1848, was seldom discriminated against in the nineteenth or early twentieth century. In fact, opposition to Jewish-Gentile marriages came more often from the Jews than from the Gentiles. Then in the 1920's the change began. Jews were systematically excluded from fashionable clubs and organized society. It is my own guess that the notorious anti-Semitism of the British in those days might have had some effect on our own traditionally copycat gentry.

All in all, Mr. Amory does remarkably well with his huge theme. As always, his anecdotes are good. I particularly like a parody composed when one of the Chicago McCormicks, eager for rejuvenation, traded glands with a young blacksmith in an operation performed by a Dr. Lespinasse: *Under the spreading chestnut tree,/The village smithy stands;/The smith a gloomy man is he;/McCormick has his glands.*

It is an interesting fact that our better writers have not written about American society at any level. They tend to confine themselves to the academic world, to the exploration of the self, to the journeyings of Americans in Schiller's "foreign cities." Only William Faulkner has composed a view of society that, despite Gothic predilections and a most curious moral vision, re-creates a social world which is and was. Richard Chase, in his study of the American novel, explaining the lack of interest in society (with or without a capital "S") defined the central form of our literature as "romance" rather than "novel." Melville, Hawthorne, the more apocalyptic work of Faulkner, all deal, he argues, with man and the cosmos, or at the very least with man and the huge wild continent he tried to master. There is a good deal of truth in Mr. Chase's theory. It is certainly true that few American writers are either equipped for or even interested in writing about the tensions between classes, the rise and fall of families, that social environment which has been and still remains the core of the British novel. By and large, only bad lady writers with three names write about "Society," and that is why Louis Auchincloss, one of our better novelists, has been so little noticed by serious-minded critics who, prepared neither by worldly experience nor by the American romance-writing of the past, tend to undervalue the novelist of — there is no other word — manners.

Mr. Auchincloss, in his latest novel, *The House of Five Talents,* demonstrates Mr. Amory's theorem of Celebrity, Society, Aristocracy. He examines a family much like the Vanderbilts; he records not so much the history of any of its members as the record of the money itself, which, finally, is often the real protagonist in America. It is a clever, good novel, and I recommend it to anyone who would like to know how life is lived or endured in the Great World. Even more to the point Mr. Auchincloss, discussing Proust in a recent issue of *Partisan Review,* made a number of observations which should be required reading for all investigators of society:

> Most people who write about society, whether they are novelists or sociologists or simply gossip columnists, make the basic error of assuming that there must be some consistency in its standards. They take for granted there are rules which govern the qualifications of those seeking admission, that if one has been gently born or if one can play polo or excel at cards or if one has the gift of pleasing or is a good shot or a good conversationalist, one may tap with confidence at any closed gate. When the rules are seen not to apply, the observer concludes that they once did, but have since broken down. As the cases of nonapplication multiply, he is apt to shrug in frustration and say: "Oh, well, nowadays it's only a question of money!" What Proust alone had the patience to piece out is that any society will apply all known standards together or individually, or in any combination needed, to include a maverick who happens to please, or to exclude an otherwise acceptable person who happens not to. Nor are society people conscious of the least inconsistency in acting so. They keep no records, and they have no written constitution. Why should their rules be defined in any way other than by a list of exceptions to them?

For the interested outsider who wants to make sense of society, "Only by conceding the arbitrariness of those on top and by intuitively sensing the bonds of congeniality that hold them together can the observer hope to appreciate the gradations in position. He must also be prepared for the bad memory of society and its habit of judging its own history by the same erroneous standards as its most misguided student." A shrewd comment, which Miss Kavaler should bear in mind.

To me, the relevant image of society is the playground: put a hundred children of the same age together, and in an hour, to the despair of the Marxist, there will be a dozen groups, each with its leader and its private games; and there will always be one particularly envied group that is thought the most agreeable, the hardest to join — and that is the highest society. Among children, liveliness, muscle and appearance matter most (very few high-school class presidents are weak or plain). The same holds true of the grown-up world where, though muscle is transmuted to money, liveliness and appearance continue to matter, often cruelly. There is also a fine element of the irrational in social arrangements. As Sir Ronald Lindsay, the British Ambassador at Washington during my childhood, said on a memorable occasion when he was being hounded by ladies desperate for invitations to his Embassy's garden party for King George VI, "I'm afraid it's all rather like Heaven; only a few are chosen." His diplomatic career collapsed on the spot, but the truth of what he said will endure forever, or at least until the money withers away.

Meanwhile, in our bored affluence, social climbing (once a secret vice) has become a favorite middle-class sport. Frankly, I'm all for it, because the climber is forced to be on his toes, to use all his cunning and resourcefulness, if he wants to make his way in the jungle gym of our society. There is no place today for the passive American of the 1940's and 1950's who used to sit home watching television, passively consuming. Action, involvement, vigor are the social climbers' characteristics. And why this sudden interest in what traditionally was a sport of the rich? Because in the shadow of the nuclear cloud, our grand old schedule of wars at twenty-five-year intervals has been deranged. But the tensions which caused those wars remain. The steam accumulates: sex, juvenile delinquency, art let off some of that steam for a few. But the best release for the many is social climbing, and social climbing, like diplomacy, is simply war conducted by other means. What, after all, is more exciting than crushing the social aspirations of another while seizing new recognition for oneself? To set one's own proud ensign on the clapboard turret of the Maidstone Club at East Hampton, declaring with middle-class Marlovian rage: "I was that climber. I was there. I made it!"

What American killer could ask for more?

[*Esquire,* June 1961.]

TWO IMMORALISTS:
ORVILLE PRESCOTT AND AYN RAND

SINCE WHAT SEEMS the original publication of *The Scarlet Letter,* the book reviews of Orville Prescott have made gaudy the otherwise impeccable grayness of the *New York Times.* Until now he has been spared criticism on the ground that since few people seriously interested in writing read him, he can neither harm nor help a literary reputation. This is certainly true, but a great many people who don't read books do read the *Times,* and, with a Prescott as view finder, their picture of American literature is distorted, to say the least.

My own objection to Mr. Prescott is not so much his style (J. Donald Adams's words are winged by comparison) or his ignorance of the more sophisticated critical strategies (he tells you the plot, anyway), but his identification with what he thinks to be his audience: the middle-aged, middle-class, moderately affluent American woman who lives in Darien, New Canaan, Scarsdale, a region bounded on the south by the Theater Guild, on the north by Womrath, on the west by Barry Goldwater and on the east by . . . Oh, well, you name it. Mr. Prescott knows that these ladies are interested in sex. He also knows that they stand firmly united in condemning all sexual activity not associated with marriage. Grimly, they attend each Tennessee Williams play so that they can complain furiously, in the lobby, that *this* time Williams has gone too far! That *this* time they are thoroughly *revolted* by that diseased mind! And never again will they expose themselves to such *filth!* And of course at the next play Williams writes they will all be back on deck, ready to be appalled again.

Now it is true that The Girls (as Helen Hokinson nicely called them) *sound* like this. It's expected of them. They don't want any trouble from one another and they have such an obvious vested interest in the family that any work which seems to accept or, worse, celebrate non-family sex presents them with a clear conflict of interest which they must resolve, at the very least, by certain ritual noises of dissent. But Mr. Prescott has missed the point to The Girls. Though they must flap when the family as an idea seems endangered, they do read more books than anyone else; they try to educate themselves politically and aesthetically; they are remarkably open-minded to new ideas; and, all in all, more tolerant of life than a great many of the husbands whose days are spent trying to make it up the ladder, lips pressed lovingly to the heel of the shoe on the next rung above. The Girls are O.K., and that is why I object so strenuously to Mr. Prescott, who deliberately anticipates and exploits their moral prejudices.

Lately, after a decade's abstinence, I have been reading Prescott again, and in a changing world it is good to know that the Good Gray Goose of the *Times* is unchanged. He still gives marks to novels not for style or insight or wisdom or art, but for "morality." Are these nice people? Is this a nice author? Adultery, pre-marital intercourse, aberration, are wicked things nice people don't do, and if an author does not firmly put them down and opt for marriage and fidelity, the offending work must go. Prescott's favorite pejorative adjective is "dull." *Lolita*, he declared with more than usual horror, was "dull, dull, dull!" Now *Lolita* was many things (there is even a case to be made against it morally, and on its own terms), but it was never dull. It was also literature, a category peculiarly mystifying to Mr. Prescott.

Recently he reviewed Alfred Duggan's new historical novel, *Family Favorites*, about Elagabalus. He tells us he admires Mr. Duggan. Now, watch. The novel "is artfully done and full of wit and irony," but it won't do, since Elagabalus "was a degenerate. His depraved orgies make tiresome and depressing reading. . . . He is not an interesting subject for a full-length novel." Well, for seventeen hundred years Elagabalus has been a fascinating subject for writers, from Dion Cassius to Gibbon, and if Duggan is really artful, witty, and ironic, I reckon he's spun a right swell yarn which is resting at this very moment on many a maple whatnot out there in Darien.

Even dizzier (and the occasion for these corrective remarks) was Mr. Prescott's review of William Brammer's political novel, *The Gay Place*. After first admiring Mr. Brammer's skill in re-creating the political scene, Mr. Prescott starts that old familiar hissing noise. He expresses wonder that young politicians commit adultery, have premarital intercourse, get drunk and otherwise behave even as people did back when Albert the Good glumly mounted Victoria to birth the Age of Guilt. Then Mr. Prescott exclaims: "Men who never dream of being faithful to their wives, who enthusiastically seduce the wives and mistresses of their friends, are faithful to standards of political conduct." He pretends to be stunned by this paradox, and that brings us to the main issue. To the average American, the word "morality" means sex, period. If you don't cheat on your wife, you're moral. It is part of our national genius to have no tradition of *public* morality. We are pleased to dismiss politics as entirely corrupt, if not financially then intellectually. Cheating the government of its taxes, and one another in business, is not only natural but necessary to survival. Now I would suggest that a man's relation to society is a matter of greater moral urgency than his sexual dealings, which, after all, are a private and relative matter. When a writer convincingly shows us, as Mr. Brammer does, young politicians devoted to right action, I am profoundly moved and morally edified. Mr. Prescott, as usual, does not recognize the moral point, preferring to root for sex.

Now, before I'm investigated for having taken the un-American stand that sex is a minor department of morality, let me try to show what I think *is* morally important.

Ayn Rand is a rhetorician who writes novels I have never been able to read. She has just published a book, *For the New Intellectual,* subtitled *The Philosophy of Ayn Rand;* it is a collection of *pensées* and arias from her novels, and it must be read to be believed. Herewith, a few excerpts from the Rand collection.

It was the morality of altruism that undercut America and is now destroying her.

Capitalism and altruism are incompatible; they are philosophical opposites; they cannot co-exist in the same man or in the same society. Today, the conflict has reached its ultimate climax; the choice is clearcut: either a new morality of rational self-interest, with its consequence of freedom . . . or the primordial morality of altruism with its consequences of slavery, etc.

Then from one of her arias for *Heldentenor*:

I am done with the monster of "We," the word of serfdom, of plunder, of misery, falsehood and shame. And now I see the face of god, and I raise this god over the earth, this god whom men have sought since men came into being, this god who will grant them joy and peace and pride. This god, this one word: "I."

The first right on earth is the right of the ego. Man's first duty is to himself.

To love money is to know and love the fact that money is the creation of the best power within you, and your passkey to trade your effort for the effort of the best among men.

The creed of sacrifice is a morality for the immoral. . . .

This odd little woman is attempting to give a moral sanction to greed and self-interest, and to pull it off she must at times indulge in purest Orwellian newspeak of the "freedom is slavery" sort. What interests me most about her is not the absurdity of her "philosophy" but the size of her audience (in my campaign for the House she was the one writer people knew and talked about). She has a great attraction for simple people who are puzzled by organized society, who object to paying taxes, who dislike the welfare state, who feel guilt at the thought of the suffering of others but who would like to harden their hearts. For them, she has an enticing prescription: altruism is the root of all evil, self-interest is the only good, and if you're dumb or incompetent that's your lookout.

She is fighting two battles. The first is against the idea of the state's being anything more than a police force and a judiciary to restrain people from stealing each other's money openly. She is in legitimate company here. But it is Miss Rand's second battle that is the moral one. She has declared war not only on Marx but on Christ. Now, although my own enthusiasm for the various systems evolved in the names of those two figures is limited, I doubt if even the most anti-Christian freethinker would want to deny the ethical value of Christ in the Gospels. To reject that Christ is to embark on dangerous waters indeed. For to justify and extol human greed and egotism is to my mind not only immoral but evil. For one thing, it is gratuitous to advise any human being to look out for himself. You can be sure that he will. It is far more difficult to persuade him to help his neighbor to build a dam or to defend a town or to give food he has accumulated to the victims of a famine. But since we must live together, dependent upon one another for many things and services, altruism is necessary to survival. To get people to do needed things is the perennial hard task of government, not to mention of religion and of philosophy. That it is right to help someone less fortunate is an idea which has figured in most systems of conduct since the beginning of the race. We often fail. That predatory demon "I" is difficult to contain, but until now we have all agreed that to help others is a right action. The dictionary definition of "moral" is "concerned with the distinction between right and wrong" as in "moral law, the requirements to which right action must conform." Though

Miss Rand's grasp of logic is uncertain, she does realize that to make even a modicum of sense she must change all the terms. Both Marx and Christ agree that in this life a right action is consideration for the welfare of others. In the one case it was through a state which was to wither away, in the other through the private exercise of the moral sense. Ayn Rand now tells us that what we have thought was right is really wrong. The lesson should have read: One for one and none for all.

Her "philosophy" is nearly perfect in its immorality, which makes the size of her audience all the more ominous and symptomatic as we enter a curious new phase in our society. Moral values are in flux. The muddy depths are being stirred by new monsters from the deep. Trolls walk the American night. Caesars are converging upon the Forum. There are storm warnings ahead. But to counter trolls and Caesars, we have such men as Lewis Mumford, whose new book, *The City in History*, inspires. He traces the growth of communities from neolithic to present times. He is wise. He is moral: that is, he favors right action and he believes it possible for us to make things better for us (not "me"). He belongs to the currently unfashionable line of makers who believe that if something is wrong it can be made right, whether a faulty water main or a faulty idea. May he flourish!

[*Esquire*, July 1961.]

EVELYN WAUGH

THE WORD "satire" is derived not from the Greek *satyr* but from the Latin phrase *satura lanx,* meaning a dish of many different foods — "antipasto" to us. The Greeks wrote satire but, significantly, they did not have a word for it. Quintilian regarded satire as Rome's unique contribution to literature. It was unintentionally named by Gaius Lucilius, who called his set of miscellaneous verses *Satirae.* A writer with a satiric bent is often best served by the less "pure" literary forms: the farce play, the picaresque novel, casual verse. In fact, today even night-club comedians like to bill themselves as satirists on the ground that any joke made at the expense of the way we live now is satiric. This is not quite the case.

A satirist is a man profoundly revolted by the society in which he lives. His rage takes the form of wit, ridicule, mockery. Aldous Huxley puts satire somewhat far down the scale of literary esthetics, making the good point that "the pure comic genius must be a great inventor" on the order, say, of Aristophanes, who created worlds, as opposed to the "mere satirist," who necessarily is rooted in *this* world. Almost by definition, the satirist does not create; he reacts to what exists with caricature and burlesque, two skills Max Beerbohm described: "Burlesque consists in the application of incongruity. Caricature consists merely in exaggeration. To burlesque a statue of Hermes, you need but put a top hat on his head. To caricature it you must exaggerate its every limb and feature." A satirist may do anything he likes to that Hermes, except carve it originally from the stone. Someone must do that for him. In the nicest sense, he is critic.

Our time's first satirist is Evelyn Waugh. For thirty years his savagery and wit have given pleasure and alarm. His mixed dish is celebrated: the Bright Young People of the Twenties, the popular press, Africa's political pretensions, death in Hollywood . . . all set down in a prose so chaste that at times one longs for a violation of syntax to suggest that its creator is fallible, or at least part American.

Yet Waugh is not a comic genius in Huxley's sense. His characters are taken from life, sometimes still struggling as he pins them to the page. He makes no new worlds. He simply turns this one inside out. He tends to look to the past for what was good rather than to the future for what might be. He is a re-actionary.

Politically, he is Tory; in religion, a Roman Catholic convert. To deal properly with the sins of the present, the satirist needs an alternative view of the way life should be. He does not need to stress it. Few satirists mean to be taken seriously as political or even moral reformers, but the alternative way must exist for them, if only as contrast. In Waugh's case that alternative is old Catholic England, where one's place was one's place and to protest it was to quarrel with God's appointment.

Ordinarily, one would do no more than note Waugh's private preferences and move on to the pleasures of his destructive art, but in recent years he will not let us off so easily. Since *Brideshead Revisited* (1945) Waugh has tended to extol his dream world at the expense of satirizing that world's implacable enemy, the twentieth century. Unfortunately, when he turns from vice to virtue, he disarms himself. His great precursor, Juvenal, preferred the old Roman Republic to the parvenu Empire, but he was too shrewd an artist to write books celebrating the political continence of Sulla or the fine austerity of Cato. He stuck to the sins of the dreadful, usable present. Waugh, however, in the military trilogy which *The End of the Battle* completes, indulges himself in romantic daydreams which are not only quite as unpleasant as the things he satirizes, but tend in their silliness to undermine his authority as critic. Juvenal would not have made that mistake.

Evelyn Waugh served in the British Army during World War II. *Men at Arms* (1952), *Officers and Gentlemen* (1955) and now *The End of the Battle* parallel Waugh's own experiences from, as he puts it, "the period of the Russo-German alliance after which the Second World War entirely changed character" (that is, the war became a Christian crusade) to the time of the Allied-Russian pact, when the war lost its holiness, ending with the Communist take-over of Yugoslavia. For this narrative Waugh has chosen a typical protagonist. Guy Crouchback belongs to one of the ancient Catholic families of England, whose seat is an old house called Broome.

When the trilogy begins, Guy is leading a solitary's existence near Genoa. He has been divorced by his wife, but he considers himself still married within the Church. The Italians do not find him sympathetic, though he is forbearing. He suffers, one would suspect, from a malady Catholics term "the arid heart." Or as Waugh puts it, "Guy had no wish to persuade or convince or to share his opinions with anyone. Even in his religion he felt no brotherhood. Often he wished that he lived in penal times when Broome had been a solitary outpost of the Faith, surrounded by aliens. Sometimes he imagined himself serving the last Mass for the last Pope in a catacomb at the end of the world." I found myself daydreaming: Evelyn Waugh and Pope John XXIII are together in the basement of an English country house. The Bomb has fallen. The human race is destroyed.

Waugh is rapturous. The Holy Father looks at him with despair. They celebrate Mass: it is *huis clos*.

Of the three volumes, *Men at Arms* is the best. Crouchback is in training. The mood of the day is caught. Despite the studied dimness of his role as Catholic gentleman, Waugh is still capable of splendid acts of destruction. Referring to Winston Churchill's broadcasts: "Guy had found them painfully boastful and they had, most of them, been immediately followed by the news of some disaster, as though in retribution from the God of Kipling's Recessional. Guy knew of Mr. Churchill only as a professional politician, a master of sham-Augustan prose, a Zionist, an advocate of the popular front in Europe, an associate of the Press Lords and of Lloyd George." Juvenal was amiable to Domitian by comparison.

Men at Arms is also remarkable for one of Waugh's finer creations, Apthorpe. He is Guy's fellow officer; a fabulist, a monomaniac — and monomania is the secret of comedic invention. Unswervingly dedicated to absurd ends, each of Apthorpe's stern consistencies adds to the comedy. His passion for his "thunder-box" and his defeat at the hands of an equally monomaniacal character, Brigadier Ritchie-Hook, display the master at his best.

Officers and Gentlemen continues the narrative from England to Alexandria to the débâcle at Crete. Accounts of military action do not suit Waugh's manner, possibly because he realizes that one man's war is another man's bore. Despite its relentless clarity, the prose often becomes perfunctory, and one starts to notice the Waugh tricks. Not since the Victorians has a writer so used mistaken identity (*Scoop* was based brilliantly on one) and coincidence. I found myself wondering if Trimmer (a cad who has been made a national hero by public-relations men) would actually meet Guy's ex-wife so neatly in Edinburgh. The British island is not that small.

One also notes a new pessimism in Waugh. Out of charity, Guy gives Apthorpe whisky in the hospital, and kills him. Though Waugh regards a virtuous act as its own reward, he seems also to suggest that no good act may have a good result in this bleak world. Like so many Catholic converts in the British literary establishment, Waugh comes perilously close to the Manichaean heresy.

The End of the Battle completes the saga of Guy Crouchback. He remarries his wife, who dies in an air raid while he is in Yugoslavia. Waugh's account of the British Communists' successful conspiracy to establish Tito is fascinating; admirers of Robert Welch's *Blue Book* will be gratified that their worst suspicions are confirmed. The Left-Wing intellectuals, Waugh's *bêtes noires* since the Thirties, get a thorough going-over. He also has some genially malicious things to say about Americans, whose speech he does not deign to record accurately (though they are from the Middle Atlantic States, they all say "I reckon").

Another target is the lower middle class. They are Waugh's Snopeses. They are everywhere, conniving, social climbing, inheriting the earth, with their terrible accents and disastrous hair. One of his characters remarks that the hair alone makes a certain plebeian insufferable. When someone remarks that the hair might be cut differently, the outraged exclaims that it is not the way the hair is cut, it is the way it *"grows!"*

In *The End of the Battle* Waugh manages to round out one final creation: Ludovic, an officer come up through the ranks; he is self-educated, enamored of words. He becomes, first, a highbrow author of *Pensées,* then a lurid best-selling novelist, mad as a hatter, talking baby talk to the Pekingese he has bought "for love." By the end of the trilogy, most of the characters are dead, briskly killed off. The few who do survive are allowed happy endings. Guy Crouchback marries a Catholic girl of ancient lineage and they live happily ever after at Broome, the future clouded only by his tendency to put on weight.

Satirists seldom end well. The rage that fills them and makes possible their irritable art is apt to turn on themselves. Dean Swift's madness is instructive. Waugh's own experiences, recorded in his extraordinary novel *The Ordeal of Gilbert Pinfold* (1956), are in that dark tradition. For Waugh's art, the difficulties inevitably increase as he turns from present horrors to his private vision of the good life. His religious and social preferences are his own business, but when he tries to make a serious case for them in his work, he is on shaky ground. Even the prose — so precise in its malice when he is on the attack — grows solemn and hollow when he tries to celebrate goodness and love and right action. One might say of him, to paraphrase James on Meredith, that he does the best things worst. Also, the snobbism, the passionate love of a lord (who can forget the dying speech of the peer in *Brideshead Revisited* as he recites his own titles to the ravishment of the Waugh protagonist?), the mean dislike of the less fortunate, tend to set one's teeth on edge.

Yet there are odd surprises and new insights. One startling turn to the screw occurs at the very end of the trilogy. Ludovic's popular novel is called *The Death Wish*, a work described by Waugh as a turning "from drab alleys of the Thirties into the odorus gardens of a recent past transformed and illuminated by disordered memory and imagination." He describes the plot. He mocks it. Why? Because the dreadful Ludovic has written *Brideshead Revisited* and Waugh has turned the full glare of his cold eye upon himself. The effect is startling, even to the comment of a literary-minded character: " 'It is an interesting thing,' said Spruce, 'but very few of the great masters of trash aimed low to start with. Most of them wrote sonnet sequences in youth. Look at Hall Caine — the protégé of Rossetti — and the young Hugh Walpole emulating Henry James. Practically no one ever sets out to write trash. Those that do don't get very far.' " Fortunately, Waugh is never trashy, and his military trilogy has much to recommend it. The wit endures; at full strength, wit is rage made bearable, and useful.

[*New York Times Book Review,* January 7, 1962.]

THE UNROCKED BOAT: SATIRE IN THE 1950'S

MALCOLM MUGGERIDGE has recently proposed that satire tends to flourish at those times when the Establishment is confident that its eternal truths and verities (to borrow Mr. Faulkner's most famous redundancy) are indeed eternal and therefore impervious to ill-natured wit. Mr. Muggeridge concludes that in an age like ours (other-directed, hydrogen-haunted, artificially tranquilized and doggedly togethered) satire is more apt to take than administer a beating. He is right in one thing: satire has taken a beating. It hardly exists in the more public art forms, and except for an occasional timid appearance in the novel or on a night-club floor, satire has seldom thrived in our comfortable land. But I suggest that the reasons for this are precisely opposite to those Mr. Muggeridge gives. In the first place, he underestimates the very real complacency of our culture, which despite lowering political weather (those atom bombs again) traditionally holds that boats in any weather are best left unrocked. Secondly, it would appear to me that satire, historically, has been most useful — and most used — when the moral and religious assumptions of a people about itself are in a state of serious confusion because of some dramatic change for good or ill in that people's fortunes.

As his world and city fell, Aristophanes attacked a demoralized war-minded Administration which did not long survive him. As the Roman Republic disintegrated, Cicero satirized radicals, Catullus satirized the mysteriously amiable Caesar, and Horace ticked off a number of highly placed bores; all this in a time of proscription and violent change. Later, under the Empire, Petronius and Lucan, though good courtiers, had the bad luck to find the Divine Nero irresistibly funny; and their satiric thrusts were rewarded with the optimum Roman prize, that ineluctable warm bath with open veins. Those were not, to say the least, complacent days. Nor can one argue that, fierce palace politics aside, the Roman imperium ever rested on certain common assumptions confidently held. Beyond a glum acceptance of law as necessary to commercial endeavor and the accidental discovery that government is largely a matter of filing and cross-indexing, the Roman state from Sulla to Constantine was gloriously confused in its morality, politics and religion. Confronted by so many rich absurdities and contradictions, satire became a high and useful art in the hands of such various men as Persius, Juvenal, Martial, even St. Paul; though between fatal baths and confinement upon disagreeable islands, the satirists themselves did not always have too good a time of it.

The Christian victory, though it did not bring peace on earth, did at least manage to put a severe leash on the satiric impulse. There are not many recorded attacks on the Church between the Emperor Julian's death and the Reformation, a millennium which — though marked by the usual wars of aggression as well as a number of religious wars (something new under the sun) — qualified supremely, in the West at least, as a period of firmly entrenched spiritual values and therefore a seedbed, one would think, for satire. Yet it was not. And the truth of the matter, of course, is that no well-organized central administration, temporal or spiritual, is apt to allow its beneficiaries the license of laughter at its own expense. Cardinals are not funny in Ireland or in Spain today, at least not publicly. Even in America, they must write particularly bad verse to occasion a wary joke or two. Yet in France and Italy, two nations which have been for some time in a state of moral and political confusion, cardinals are stock figures of comedy, cropping up in numerous jokes, good and bad, malicious and amiable. I worry the Roman Church only because it is an elderly institution of great significance morally and therefore an obvious target for useful satire. At present, in America, it is not.

Now I would propose that the United States in its short history has been much too preoccupied uniting and exploring, pioneering and building, inventing and consuming, to give much thought to anything not relevant to the practical and immediate. Not that we have lacked for harsh critics. In fact, most of our country's better writers have been nay-sayers, deploring the day and resolutely pessimistic about tomorrow. On the other hand, our humorists have been jolly and ubiquitous. We all know, rather wearily, about frontier humor. Mark Twain's jokes go on and on and some are funny but none is truly satiric because he was not one to rock the boat. It was his ordeal to be tamed, and the petulance and bitterness of his final book, *What Is Man?*, answers as nothing else could why he did not dare question any of his society's basic assumptions.

Henry James observed that it took a great deal of history to make a little bit of literature. I suspect it takes a far more homogeneous, more settled, yet more uneasy society to produce satirists. And if one is to be met by the argument that God forbid things should be any worse simply to make matters easier for one small department of literature, I would be the first to agree that the benign incompetence of the Great Golfer and his Team is certainly preferable to a touchy Nero or to an inscrutable Caesar.

Yet there is a real need for the satirist in our affairs, especially now. Since the Second World War and its horrors there has been a remarkable change in our society. Anti-Semitism seems happily to have vanished, except among the more irritable Jews, while anti-Catholics no longer smile, at least in mixed religious company, when the Vatican certifies that the sun did a dance over Portugal. Even my Southern relatives employ a certain tact in discussing the Problem. A profound tolerance is in the land, a tolerance so profound that it is not in its effect entirely unlike terror. One dare not raise one's voice against any religion, idea or even delinquency if it is explicable by a therapist. I suspect that much of the American's hatred of Russia and Communism is simply a siphoning off of other irrational dislikes which, blocked by the stern tolerance of the day, can find expression only in Communist baiting. I do not propose that we return to the bad old days of holding people responsible for inherited characteristics. Yet I should like to have tolerance learned from within and not have it imposed from without. To put forward a recklessly unsympathetic proposition: As long as any group within the society deliberately maintains its identity, it is, or should be, a fair target for satire, both for its own good and for the society's. Laughing at someone else is an excellent way of learning how to laugh at oneself; and questioning what seem to be the absurd beliefs of another group is a good way of recognizing the potential absurdity of many of one's own cherished beliefs; witness the travels of Gulliver.

It is generally agreed and officially lamented that we are in a new age of conformity. Youth wants security,

not adventure. The great questions are not asked because the realization that there are no absolute answers
has at last penetrated to the bottom layer of society —
and why be curious if the answers are only tentative?
Now, if this time is indeed so bland, then according to
Muggeridge's law, satire must flourish. Yet satire hardly
exists. In perfect comfort the squares grow ever more
rectilinear. And to strike the minatory note, if ever there
was a people ripe for dictatorship it is the American
people today. Should a homegrown Hitler appear,
whose voice, amongst the public orders, would be
raised against him in derision? Certainly no voice on
television: "Sorry, the guy has a lot of fans. Sure, we
know he's bad news, but you can't hurt people's feelings.
They buy soap, too." And elsewhere there would be
the tolerant reflex: "Well, he *could* be right. After all, a
lot of people seem to agree with him . . ." And then
the iron fist closes, and we start *our* Empire.

I have often chided my Soviet friends on the naïveté
of their country's censorship. Newly literate and still
awed by the printed word, the Russian governors are
terrified of ideas. If only they knew what our governors
know: that in a massive egalitarian society no idea
which runs counter to the prevailing superstitions can
successfully penetrate the national carapace. We give
our solemn critics every freedom, including the one to
fail to be heard. And fail they do: silence and indifference neutralize the irritant more effectively than brain-
washing. Yet this age could be a marvelous one for

satirists. Look at the targets: Christianity, Psychiatry, Marxism, Romantic Love, Xenophobia, Science (all capitalized and all regarded with reverence if not admiration). You need only take your pick, and not worry about bad taste. If one can make the cautious laugh by clowning, half the work is done, for laughter is the satirist's anaesthetic: he can then make his incision, darting on before the audience knows what has been done to it. But he must be swift and engaging, or the laughter will turn to indifferent silence, the ultimate censorship.

Where can the American satirist operate today? Not on television, seldom if ever in the movies, and on the stage only if he is willing to play the buffoon. But the novel remains; and it would be good to see those writers with a talent for satire (Randall Jarrell for one) strike boldly at the large targets, without that vitiating diffidence peculiar to the contempoary American novelist. We don't know very much, they seem to say; we are deep of course, often mystic, and we do know that love and compassion are the most beautiful things in the world and in our studies of loneliness we like to show the full potentiality of love (how Flaubert would have satirized these latter-day Bovarists!), but we don't know or want to know any senators, bishops or atomic scientists; as for psychiatrists — well, we like ours: he is a Jungian. Shrinking each into his own skin, our novelists grow more private, and for those who lack genius (the majority) more dull. I do not suggest that everyone turn his hand to satire. It is, after all, only one of a number of ways to get the thing said. Nor do I echo those solid *Forsyte Saga* newspaper reviewers who maintain that what we need is a good novel about the wool trade or building a dam, but what I feel we do need is more engagement in the outer world. And daring. And wit. And, finally, satirists, who are needed as truth is needed — for is not satire, simply, truth grinning in a solemn canting world?

[The *Nation,* April 26, 1958.]

PERSONAL

WRITING PLAYS FOR TELEVISION

U<small>NTIL</small> I <small>BEGAN</small> to write plays for television, I entertained an amiable contempt for my stagestruck playwright friends who so meekly (masochistically, I thought) submitted their talents to the irrelevant strictures of directors and stars, of newspapermen in Wilmington and of sudden, brief acquaintances in hotel rooms. I had taken to heart the failure of the prose writer in the theater. From Smollett's irritable attempts to get his tragedy produced to Henry James as he was jeered from the stage on his first night, the novelist has cut a ponderous, sad figure beneath the proscenium arch. As a novelist, I was wary, preferring to suffer my reverses and petty triumphs on the familiar ground of prose and *not* in the theater, strewn already with the corpses of illustrious confrères.

The reason for our party's failure in what should have

been a natural arena is caught in Flaubert's phrase: "The theater is not an art but a secret." And the secret is deceptively simple: dialogue is not prose. It is another language, and a talent for the novel does not necessarily mean a talent for the theater. The novel is the more private and (to me) the more satisfying art. A novel is all one's own, a world fashioned by a single intelligence, its reality in no way dependent upon the collective excellence of others. Also the mountebankery, the plain showmanship which is necessary to playwriting, strikes the novelist as disagreeably broad. One must show *every* collision on the stage, while in the novel it is often a virtue to avoid the obvious scene, to come at the great moments obliquely. Even dialogue is not the same in a novel as it is on the stage. Seldom can dialogue be taken from a book and played by actors. The reason is one of pace rather than of verisimilitude. Certainly, in our country, most novelists have an accurate ear for speech; it is a gift liberally bestowed upon the good and the bad alike, the gray badge of naturalism. Yet in the novel, *duration* differs from the stage. The novelist's arrangement of dialogue is seldom as concentrated as the playwright's, whose line must finally be achieved by people talking, unassisted by an author's stage management.

Aware of the essential difference between the novel and the play, I kept happily to my own country until the black winter of 1953, when I realized in a moment of revelation that the novel as a popular art form had come to a full halt. There were many reasons. Television had stunned it. The new critics had laid it out all neat in a blue suit, a flower in its waxy hands (HERE LIES THE NOVEL, EXPLICATED), and their funeral orations were already under way in the literary quarterlies. The newspaper reviewers, lagging in their serene way some twenty years behind the fact, wanted more Kipling and less art, while the public, its attention distracted by television and the movies, firmly refused to pay five dollars for anyone's novel, aware that if a book contained enough healthy American sadism they could eventually buy it in a cheap paperback edition. By 1953, unpopular novelists like myself were living precariously on the bounty of reprint publishers; a bounty which ended when those jolly opportunists flooded the newsstands, sinking many, both good and bad. Needless to say, none of this happened quickly. Disaster approached with stealthy tread, and not until my revelation did I awaken to the harshness of the situation: that I was on the verge of providing future thesis writers ("Ah, yes, Gore Vidal . . . perhaps, Haskins, *you* can make something of him, though I liked your first project better. I mean, Caroline poetry is something you can get your teeth into") with a poignant page or two of metropolitan suffering, before I went off to Africa to run rifles, never to be seen again.

But happily, when faced with ruin, all one's cunning and resourcefulness rush to the surface, and if one's career is conducted beneath a beneficent star, crisis is healthy. I looked about me. I had been a novelist for a decade. I had been hailed as the peer of Voltaire, Henry James, Jack London, Ronald Firbank and James T. Farrell. My early, least satisfactory works had been best-sellers. Though not yet thirty years old, I was referred to in the past tense, as one of those novelists of the 1940's from whom so much had been expected.

I turned to my peers to see what they were doing. I discovered that the most colorful was writing unsuccessful musical comedies and the most talented had virtuously contrived to die. The others had dropped from view, most of them finding dim employment either in anonymous journalism or in the academy. The cleverest ones had married rich wives and traveled a lot. The prospect was not flooded with light.

But one must live, as they say, and since I do not write popular short stories or journalism, or teach, and since I was spoiled by ten years of receiving money for the work I would have done whether I had been paid or not (the happiest of lives and the luckiest), it looked very much as if I should have to turn to the fantasy world of business and get a job. At that crucial moment, I discovered television.

I had not watched television until the winter I decided to write for it. At the time, its great advantage for me was proximity. I live on the bank of the Hudson, and there to the south, in New York City, was this fine source of revenue. I was intrigued. I was soon enthralled. Right off, there is the immediacy of play-writing. There they are, one's own creations, fleshed out by living people, the symbolic detail isolated by the camera as millions of strangers in their homes watch one's private vision made public. The day after my debut in February of 1954, I was committed seriously to writing for the camera. I discovered that although the restrictions imposed by a popular medium are not always agreeable, they do at least make creative demands upon one's euphemistic talents. More often than not, the tension between what one is not allowed to say and what one must say creates ingenious effects which, given total freedom, might never have been forced from the imagination. The only analogy I can think of is the nineteenth-century novel. Nearly all the productions of that extraordinary age were published first in magazines edited for gentlewomen and supervised by Mrs. Grundy, her fist full of asterisks. There was so much the harried novelist could *not* say that he was impelled to freight heavily what he *could* say with other meanings, accomplishing the great things by indirection, through association and logical echo.

The same is true now in television. With patience and ingenuity there is nothing that the imaginative writer cannot say to the innocent millions. Of course the naturalistic writer has a more difficult time. He is used to making his point directly and bluntly: *You are a slut.* And he is morose when he cannot bluntly hammer out the obvious, the way he could on the stage or in the lower novel. But for my kind of second-story work, television is less confining. Also, the dramatic art is particularly satisfying for any writer with a polemical bent; and I am at heart a propagandist, a tremendous hater, a tiresome nag, complacently positive that there is no human problem which could not be solved if people would simply do as I advise. This sort of intensity, no matter how idiotic, works well in the drama if only because there is nothing more effective than having something to say.

As for the world of television, the notable characteristics are youth and enthusiasm. The dramatists, directors and producers are all young men, and their deep pleasure in this new toy is communicable and heartening. There is none of the bored cynicism one often finds in Hollywood studios, nor any of the rapacity and bad temper endemic to the theater in New York. Most television plays are bad, but considering that television uses up hundreds of new plays a year and that there have not been a hundred fine plays written in the last two thousand years, they can be excused their failures if their intentions are honorable. And at the moment, the very real sense of honor the better television writers possess lends excitement to their work.

Another novelty for me has been working with people. I had never before worked with anyone, and the thought of belonging to a group was unnerving. But to my surprise I enjoyed it. Working on a play is not unlike being stranded on an island with a group of strangers from a foundered ship's company. For ten days, actors, director, author, technicians work together, getting to know one another almost morbidly well. Then, when the play is over, sadly, sweetly, the players and the management separate, never to meet again — until the next play together.

A play on television of the sort I write is not filmed. It is seen on the air at the exact moment it is performed. The actors build their performances as they would on the stage. The only difference is that they are being photographed by three cameras and we, the audience, are watching a play as though it were a movie.

In the last two years I have written nearly twenty plays. All but seven were either half-hour plays or adaptations. Incidentally, adapting is neither easier nor more difficult than writing an original play. There is, I think, only one basic trick to it: simply knowing how to read precisely and critically. One must get the point of the work. I make this obvious comment because just as literary men are seldom playwrights, playwrights are almost never literary men, and they are usually baffled and bored by the slower, denser order of the novel. In fact, excepting the poet-dramatists, there is a good case that the drama is not literature at all but an entirely separate art requiring collective means to achieve its moments, sharing with prose nothing beyond the general human preoccupation. A gift for playwriting is only a form of cleverness, like being adept at charades or Double-Crostics, while novel writing goes, at its best, beyond cleverness to that point where one's whole mind and experience and vision *are* the novel and the effort to translate this wholeness into prose *is* the life: a circle of creation.

Of course it can be argued that a Shaw or a Chekhov achieves a comparable wholeness in the theater, but the very exceptionalness of any play which is better than viable suggests the narrow boundaries of a literary form whose effectiveness depends as much on interpretation as on the line written, the idea proposed, the light cast. We have all been moved by plays whose productions led us to believe that truth had rent the air about us, only to find later, upon reading the script, that we were tricked, or rather *served* beautifully, in the theater by a number of talents of which the writer's was but one, and perhaps the least.

There are a number of mechanical limitations in television which time may eliminate. For instance, a play done "live" is seen only once, and that is the end. So many fine performances, so many good plays written on air, with nothing to show for all the work done but a kinescope (a filmed record of the play) that because of labor-union and technical considerations may not be shown again on television. It is a waste of many talents. Someday, perhaps on the new magnetic tape, a play which is broadcast live will be accurately recorded and reshown.

One would also like to see a repertory system in television, not only for the actors of course (television *is* a kind of repertory for actors, providing the talented with work and experience) but for the redoing of plays whose value has been established; and there are now a number of interesting plays to choose from. Finally, waiting in the wings, is something called subscription television. Certain productions will be available only to those viewers who pay to see them, a miraculous state of affairs for the writer, who will then have an audience which in a sense is *his* and not accidental. Also, he will be free of those nervous men the advertisers, who now largely control television.

All things considered, I suspect that the Golden Age for the dramatist is at hand. There is so much air to be illustrated, so many eyes watching, so much money to be spent, so many fine technicians and interpreters at one's command, that the playwright cannot but thrive. As for myself? I am writing prose again.*

[*New World Writing* #10, 1956.]

* See Note 9 in the Appendix.

PUTTING ON "VISIT TO A SMALL PLANET"

I AM NOT AT HEART a playwright. I am a novelist turned temporary adventurer; and I chose to write television, movies, and plays for much the same reason that Henry Morgan selected the Spanish Main for his peculiar — and not dissimilar — sphere of operations. The reasons for my conversion to piracy are to me poignant, and to students of our society perhaps significant.

If I may recall in nostalgic terms the near past, I began writing novels at the end of the Second World War. Those were the happy years when a new era in our letters was everywhere proclaimed. We would have, it was thought, a literature to celebrate the new American empire. Our writers in reflecting our glory would complement the beautiful hardness of our currency. But something went wrong. The new era did not materialize and the work of my generation was dismissed — for the present at least — as a false dawn. It is a fact that the novel as a popular art form retrogressed gravely in our reign. Not clever enough to interest the better critics or simple enough to divert the public, we lost the critics to pure criticism and the public to impure television. By the 1950's I and my once golden peers were plunged into that dim cellar of literature characterized as "serious," where, like the priests of some shattered god, we were left to tend our prose privately: so many exiles, growing mushrooms in the dark.

The passage of time has only confirmed the new order. Less and less often is that widening division between the commercially viable and the seriously meaningful bridged by the rare creator who is both. Most of the large publishing events of recent years have been the crudely recollected experiences of nonwriters. Lost is the old conception of the man of letters creating a life's work to be enjoyed by the common reader in continuity. True, that nineteenth-century phenomenon never quite took root in this country; for lovely though New England's Indian summer was, winter when it came was killing. Nowadays, our better literary men seek refuge in the universities, leaving what is left of the public novel to transient primitives and to sturdy hacks. Nor, let me say, are the serious writers themselves responsible for their unpopularity, as our more chauvinistic editorial writers would have it. The good work of the age is being done, as always. Rather it is the public which has changed. Television, movies, the ease of travel . . . so many new diversions have claimed the attention of that public which once read that I think it doubtful if the novel will ever again have the enormous prestige, the universal audience it enjoyed that fine morning when an idler on a Mississippi wharf shouted to the pilot of a passing steamer: "Is Little Nell dead?" And, alas, Mistah Kurtz, he dead, too; solemnly embalmed by the Academy.

Today, the large audience holds communion in a new, more compelling establishment. I doubt if many Americans could identify a single character in a work of modern fiction, but there are few who could not describe in exact detail the latest comedian's joke on television. Yet it is vain to deplore a cultural change. If after two pre-eminent centuries the novel no longer is useful to the public, only novelists need mourn, for it is a fact of civilization that each society creates the games it wants to play and rejects those it regards as irrelevant.

The main audience has turned back to the play (in all its various forms, both "live" and filmed). Nevertheless, it is a stoic consolation for those of us whose first allegiance is to the novel to know that there will always be some serious interest in one's work and that the keys to the kingdom of prose will continue to be passed on from hand to hand. And though I rather suspect that in a century's time the novel will be as rare and private an art form as poetry today or that delicate and laborious process by which dedicated men fire glass with color, it will always be worth the doing.

Over the years I attempted three stage plays. When I was nineteen I wrote a quasi-poetical work about, Heaven alone knows why, a man who became a werewolf in Manhattan. I destroyed all copies of this early effort only to learn recently that a collector has somehow got hold of a copy, a ghastly prospect for some as yet unborn English major.

The next play I wrote was on an equally obscure subject, written in a frenzy in the spring of 1948 at Shepheard's Hotel in Cairo. Later that summer, I gave it to Tennessee Williams to read. He pronounced it the worst play he'd read in some time, and I abandoned playwriting for good, I thought, after first pointing out to him that a literary form which depended on the combined excellence of others for its execution could hardly be worth the attention of a serious writer, adding with deliberate cruelty that I did not envy him being stagestruck and his life taken up with such frivolous people as actors and directors. He agreed that I should not expose myself just yet to this sort of tedium.

Six years later, driven by necessity, I took the plunge into television, the very heart of darkness, and to my surprise found that I liked it. But despite television's raw youth there is a tradition already firmly established that comedies seldom work on the small screen and that satire never does. Like most traditions, this one is founded on a part truth. For one thing, the comedy timing of stage-trained actors is inevitably affected by the absence of human response during a performance, and for another several people sitting at home glumly staring at a television set are not apt to find anything very amusing unless it is heavily underscored by laughter from a studio audience. And plays on television are performed without audiences.

Satire presents a further difficulty for the mass audience. If satire is to be effective, the audience must be aware of the thing satirized. If they are not, the joke falls flat. Unfortunately for our native satirists, the American mass audience possesses very little general information on any subject. Each individual knows his own immediate world, but, as various research polls continually inform us, he holds little knowledge in common with others. Even political jokes, if they were allowed on television, would not have much relevance. Recently one national poll disclosed that almost half of those queried could not identify the Secretary of State. The size of the population has much to do with this collective ignorance. When Aristophanes made a satiric point, he could be confident that his audience would appreciate his slyest nuance because in a small community each citizen was bound to share with his fellows a certain amount of general information — literary, religious, and political. National units today are too large and, in America at least, education too bland to hope for much change. As a result, satire, unless done very broadly, like that of Al Capp, our national Hogarth (or the playing version of my *Visit to a Small Planet*), puzzles and irritates rather than amuses.

I have often thought that the domination of naturalism in our letters is directly attributable to the breakdown of the old homogeneous American society of the nineteenth century, caused by the influx of immigration, the discovery of exciting new machinery, the ease of travel. Before this burst of population and invention, an educated man, writing allusively, could assume that his readers would respond knowledgeably to a fairly large number of references both literary and social. Since 1900 this has been less and less possible, and it is no coincidence that naturalism should be to this day the preferred manner in the novel, if only because the naturalistic writer, by definition, takes nothing for granted. He assumes that the reader knows no more than he chooses to tell. He constructs a literal world of concrete detail. His narrative is easily followed. He records the surface of life with a photographer's care, leaving the interpretation, the truth of his record, to the reader's imagination. The result is that our time's most successful *popular* writing is journalism, another dagger at the novel's heart.

The idea for *Visit to a Small Planet* (from outer space arrives a charming hobbyist named Kreton whose blithe intent it is to start a war: "I mean it's the one thing you people down here do *really* well!") was rejected by three television sponsors before Philco-Goodyear Playhouse bought it. I was told that the advertisers found the premise alarming, which was certainly disingenuous of them. Had I not spun my fragile satire about the one glittering constant in human affairs, the single pastime that never palls: war? In fact, one might say that *Visit* is the happiest of pro-war plays.

But only Philco saw the austere beauty of this conceit, and on the night of May 8, 1955, it was telecast. With some anxiety we waited for the roof to fall in. To our very real surprise it did not, and most people were pleased with the result. I was then informed that a producer would like me to do a stage version for Broadway. And so it came to pass. Expansion was not difficult. As a novelist, I was accustomed to using a hundred thousand words to net my meaning. My problem theatrically has always been one of compression.

After the script was ready there were the usual trials, delays, problems of temperament; each participant convinced that the others had gone into secret league to contrive his professional ruin (and on occasion cabals did flourish, for the theater is a child's world).

On January 16, 1957, the play opened in New Haven. From that moment until the New York opening on February 7, I was more dentist than writer, extracting the sharper (and not always carious) teeth. The heart of the play's argument was a scene in the second act between Kreton and the Secretary-General of the United Nations. At each performance the audience, charmed by the fooling that had gone before, grew deathly cold as the debate began. This was not what they had anticipated (a fault, I own, of the dramaturgy), and their confidence in the play was never entirely regained. A few days before we left Boston, I replaced the scene with a lighter one, involving the principals and giving the curtain to our subtlest player, the cat. The substitute was engaging; the play moved amiably; no one was shocked. (Earlier, some observers in New Haven had declared the entire conception unwholesomely menacing. If only they had seen the first draft of the play, in which I blew up the whole world at the end, the perfect curtain!) So by deliberate dulling of the edge of the satire, the farce flourished.

A number of reviewers described the play as a vaudeville, a very apt description and one in which I concur, recalling a letter from Bernard Shaw to Granville-Barker: "I have given you a series of first-rate music hall entertainments thinly disguised as plays, but really offering the public a unique string of turns by comics and serio-comics of every popular type." That of course is only half the truth, but it is the charming half. In the case of *Visit,* the comedic approach to the theme tended to dictate the form. Having no real commitment to the theater, no profound convictions about the well-made or the ill-made play, I tend to write as an audience, an easily bored audience. I wrote the sort of piece I should like to go to a theater to see, one in which people say and do things that make me laugh. And though monsters lurk beneath the surface, their presence is sensed rather than dramatically revealed. My view of reality is not sanguine, and the play for all its blitheness turns resolutely toward a cold night. Fortunately for the play's success, the incisors were extracted out of town and the venture was a hit. But in that word "hit" lies the problem.

I was obliged to protect an eighty-thousand-dollar investment, and I confess freely that I obscured meanings, softened blows, and humbly turned wrath aside, emerging with a successful play which represented me very little. It is not that what was fashioned was bad or corrupt; I rather fancy the farce we ended up with, and I think it has a good deal of wear in it. But the play that might have been, though hardly earthshaking, was far more interesting and true. Like too many others I played the game stolidly according to rules I abhorred, realizing that the theater and its writers are seriously, perhaps fatally, hampered by economic pressure. Because it costs too much to put on a play, one works in a state of hysteria. Everything is geared to success. Yet art is mostly failure. It is only from a succession of daring, flawed works that the occasional masterwork comes. But in the Broadway theater to fail is death, and in an atmosphere so feverish it is difficult to work with much objectivity. Only the honest hacks have a good time of it. Cannily, they run up a banner: It's just us again, kids, trying to make a buck. And they are let off with genial contempt. It is the crankier, more difficult writers who must work at a disadvantage, and efforts to divert them into familiar safe channels are usually disastrous. Is there a solution? I see none; unless it be the decentralization of the theater to the smaller cities and to the universities, where the means of production will be less than good but the freedom greater, particularly the luxurious freedom to fail.

[The *Reporter*, July 11, 1957.]

A NOTE ON "THE BEST MAN"

W<small>HEN IT IS</small> ninety in the shade and the Hudson River has gone dull gray and I cross a certain bit of lawn contained by river wall, mysteriously a train of associations is set off: I brood on Henry James. I fret about Strether. I deplore the Princess and her treatment of Hyacinth and (though ripeness is all and the rest is the madness of art) I wonder if, really, I am taken with James's way. Is he too neat? too artificial? too classical? too much devoted to balance? Item: *The Tragic Muse*. Each of four characters begins at the farthest extremity of an "X." They cross. Each ends in an opposite position. One wonders: does a living pulse beat, or is it only a metronome?

One day last July, the temperature went to ninety. The river turned a sullen gray. I crossed the brown lawn and started, irritably, to rethink *The Tragic Muse*. No,

I did not like the method, I decided. It was all a trick, an easy parlor game. As if one were, in contemporary terms, to take — just for example — a man of exemplary private but monstrous public life and contrast him to a man of "immoral" private and exemplary public life. That was just the sort of thing James would take on. How he would enjoy mechanically turning the screw upon each character! For sake of argument, one might make the two men politicians, perhaps fighting one another for the Presidency. Then demonstrate how, in our confused age, immorality means, simply, sex found out. To most Americans, cheating, character assassination, hypocrisy, self-seeking are taken for granted as the way things are — not pleasant, perhaps, but: Son, you've got to look after Number One, because there's a lot of competition. . . . By the time I got back to the house to escape the sun and *The Tragic Muse* revisited, I had the characters for *The Best Man*. One very perceptive (if not very flattering) critic recently compared me to Sardou, remarking how I displayed the same dramatic artifice, the well-madeness, the somewhat mechanical balance. The critic was right in his intuition, because who did study Sardou devoutly, and disastrously? Not I but Henry James, my instructor.

For once, however, I did not write. I thought. I had the general line of the play clear in my head. Narrative time would be concentrated to the three days preceding a nominating convention. I planned short scenes, alternating between the candidates' suites in a Philadelphia hotel. Yet I had still to make up my mind about the two important issues on which the plot would turn. First: What in William Russell's past could the opportunist Senator Cantwell use at the last minute which might effectively end his candidacy? Second: What might Russell find in Cantwell's private life which would, first, stop Cantwell and, second and morally more important, revolt Russell in the doing?

It was Richard Rovere who gave me the answer to the first: intimations of mental instability. It was a valuable suggestion. The *Zeitgeist* is full now of the buzz of psychoanalysis. Everyone's mind is cluttered with at least a few misunderstood clinical phrases and conceptions. If William Russell had once had a nervous breakdown and Senator Cantwell were to get his hands on Russell's case history and threaten to reveal the contents to the delegates at the convention, it was unlikely Russell could survive politically. A Presidential candidate can have many faults, but even a hint of mental instability is disqualifying. The second problem I solved reluctantly. What could be brought up about Senator Cantwell? I wanted something ambiguous: it might or it might not be true, but, true or not, Russell must resent having to reveal it, even to save himself. This was limiting. If Cantwell had stolen money, got a girl aborted, run away in battle, taken dope, or been a Communist or a member of the Ku Klux Klan, Russell might be reluctant to bring up the matter but he would certainly not hesitate, to save himself, especially if he were convinced the charges were true. Homosexuality was about the only thing left. It was a charge which, true or not, Russell would detest exploiting. It was also an ironic charge to bring against Cantwell, whose marriage was deliberately made in that heaven where Rose Franken's Claudia and David were created. Once these two matters were decided, I was able to write the play in three weeks.

I use the theater as a place to criticize society, to satirize folly, to question presuppositions. Kenneth Tynan has remarked that in this play I was not "adventurous" politically (i.e., Marxist) and at my best only as a destructive satirist — but who is not? It is infinitely harder to ask questions in such a way that the audience is led, not to answers (the province of the demagogue), but to new perceptions. No writer's ultimate conclusions are ever of much interest, if only because wisdom, when concentrated, is proverbial. Shaw's conclusions about the Life Force (appropriated from Bergson) are not very helpful, but his method of questioning and burlesquing is his art, and at his best he teases his audience into asking the right questions. For myself, I can think of no other reason to write plays, though other writers have other incentives, equally useful.*

[*Theatre Arts*, July 1960.]

* See Note 10 in the Appendix.

APPENDIX

1. NOTE TO "John Kennedy: A Translation for the English"

When John Kennedy was elected President, I wrote Mrs. Kennedy that though I was tempted to write about him, I would restrain myself because I wanted very much for him to be great, and knowing my own satiric impulse, I felt that nothing I was apt to put down on paper would be helpful. I have kept to my promise in the United States. But when the British *Sunday Telegraph* (then a new, now a most successful paper) asked me to describe him for its readers, I said that I would. . . . But not so much as a critic (which I would have to be, in America) as a translator of character.

If nothing else, the piece reflects accurately the early euphoric days of the Administration, before the Cuban debacle. I am told what I wrote was well regarded in England for exactly two weeks. Then the Cuban crisis began and I was promptly abandoned, along with my belaureled hero, both scuttled in the Bay of Pigs. The wisdom I had claimed for him had not been demonstrated and my estimate of his ability was dismissed as hyperbole, for now. Nevertheless, I take back nothing. Kennedy is capable; he is dedicated; he is the best-trained man to become President in this century. But he is faced not only with our own declining power in the world but, worse, our declining will to assume responsibility in our own society as well as in the world. Great forces block him at every turn. His field of maneuver *vis-à-vis* the Soviet is the narrowest in which any President has had to operate. If we are embarked upon tragedy, it will be ironic that a man as capable and as devoted as he should have been navigator to the West.

Mrs. Kennedy's stepfather, Hugh D. Auchincloss, was my stepfather, and we share a half-brother and a half-sister. We all grew up, but at different times, at Merrywood, the Auchincloss house in Virginia. I lived there from the age of ten until sixteen. Jackie then moved in at the age of eleven. That house, for good and ill, has had great effect upon those whose childhood was spent there and someday (*after* the Kennedy Administration) I shall write about it. But for now I keep to my promise. Translation, yes; analysis, no.

2. NOTE TO "Barry Goldwater: A Chat"

I could not have been more startled. An editor at *Life* wanted to know if I would like to write a piece for them on Senator Barry Goldwater. I said of course I

would like to do it, but didn't *Life* know that I
would . . . ? Yes, they knew. They would present the
piece with fair warning to their readers: a liberal examines a conservative. I could write whatever I chose.
Needless to say, I was dubious. One of the prevailing
demons of our intellectual Establishment is Luce journalism. Novel after novel has been published showing
sensitive liberals crushed in that vast *Time-Life* machine of reaction. I daresay there is some truth in all
these novels, though I tend to side with Hemingway,
who, when asked if he thought writing journalism,
movies, was hurtful to the artist, shrugged and said:
"Every whore finds his vocation for life." The politics
of Henry Luce could hardly hurt any employee, unless
that employee chooses to be hurt. Economic dependence
on writing for hire might eventually sap his initiative,
but isn't that a choice? Is the writer perhaps, if not a
whore, an injustice collector? In any case, I was forced
to re-examine the *Time-Life* myth in the light of my
own experience. I was not interfered with. I wrote exactly what I wanted to write. *Life's* research is extraordinary in its thoroughness. There was no censorship,
and there were no experiments with my sentences.

As for Senator Barry Goldwater, I found him exactly
as I have written about him. I used the interview device instead of the straight critique, knowing that it is
always easier to catch the eye of the mass audience with
dialogue and proper names and familiar details. I
wanted, plainly, to influence those who were unde-

cided about the Senator. The best attack to date on his position was written by Gilbert A. Harrison in the *New Republic*. But I am sure that piece had no practical effect: those who liked the Senator would dismiss it as partisan, while those who disliked him (the readers of the *New Republic*) didn't need to be confirmed in their hostility. It is for the ones in between that I wrote.

I must have got close to home, for the fury of the Right wing was heartening. Editorials were written denouncing me. I also got many touching letters from Arizona, where the Right wing apparently has created a small reign of terror. One woman wrote that she and her family were moving back to the East after ten years. Along with other liberals they had been branded as Communists and socially ostracized — all this the work of a small but vigorous group of do-badders. The organized mail to me and to *Life* was plentiful and bristling with paranoia. How could one tell which letters had been organized? Because they all used the word "innuendo."

Personally, I am told that the Senator took the line of being more sinned against than sinning, commenting, however, with some irritability that there was more about me in the article than there was about him — a shrewd criticism. But then that was to be the nature of the piece: an "impossible interview" of the *Vanity Fair* sort.

For reasons of space I had to cut one of my favorite stories. I asked the Senator if he knew Ayn Rand. Yes, he knew her. They were pen pals but he found it hard to keep up with her as a correspondent because she was in the habit of writing him twelve-page letters. "We have one basic difference of opinion, though." He looked very solemn. "You see, I see a place for God in the scheme of things, and she doesn't." As a Senator I wish Goldwater well. He has a radical, almost anarchist turn of mind that is very beguiling at a time when safe, canting liberalism is the rule. As a President of course he would be a disaster.

Writing these words I wonder: How interesting will a piece of this sort be in twenty years, in a hundred years, if read by someone who knows neither the subject nor the era? Ideally, even political journalism should have some lasting relevance. I doubt very much that these pages will be of more than antiquarian interest: a minor politician, characteristic of his time . . . unless this should be, as I suspect it is, a climactic time in the country's life, an end and a beginning. In that case, even the peripheral men of state will be interesting. Two millennia have passed, yet we still know Cassius.

3. NOTE TO "Closing the Civilization Gap"

Many people wrote me demanding to know: Who was the policeman? What had been done? What could *they* do? Shortly after the piece appeared in *Esquire*, a reporter from the *Washington Post and Times-Herald* telephoned me. He was at police headquarters. He wanted to know who the night editor was I had spoken to, and what name the plainclothesman had given me. I told him the day and the time I had called the *Post*. He would have to find out who was on duty then. I gave him the policeman's name. I also told him that I would give him the taxicab driver's license number if he would call back the next day. He said that he would, but he did not; and that was the end of that.

4. NOTE TO "The Commercialites"

Since Jerome Lawrence is an acquaintance of mine and a most amiable man, I suffered real discomfort in giving him such a bad notice. And this, by the way, is the most difficult part of being a critic. What do you do about people you like whose work is not good? As the late President Harding would say: "Don't knock; boost!" I do believe (perhaps wrongly) that I lack sadism. I am positive I get no pleasure out of hurting others in print. Yet if one is not scrupulously accurate in recording impressions there is no point to writing. I was disturbed a few years ago when gossip columnists tried to create a "feud" between Arthur Miller and me as a result of "Love Love Love." I don't know Mr. Miller. I admire Mr. Miller. In a certain context I dealt with him severely for his pretensions while praising his true talent. I had put, finally, the blame for his failure (as well as for my own) on the society we live in. Beyond a point no one can transcend the period to which he belongs (like that ninth-century French bishop who at the end of a crude but oddly beautiful letter apologizes for the poorness of his Latin, because "we have no longer civilization"). But in the world of the Commercialites, all is personal. If you knock, it is either out of revenge or envy. Good guys boost.

In any case, I was not happy at having dealt so harshly with *The Gang's All Here*. To ease my conscience and to learn more about the subject, I started reading biographies of Harding and I have a part-apology to make to Lawrence and Lee. They did not exaggerate. Harding was, in many ways, even more fatuous than the character shown us on the stage. He was also a near-tragic figure in a completely American way. It was his madness to want to be loved at any cost. He sacrificed everything to this one prevailing passion, and nearly wrecked our government in the doing. He perished broken and puzzled, a Willy Loman, lusting only to be well-liked. Harding is a theme for tragedy, and the fault of this now forgotten play is largely the absence of any point of view about him. Lawrence and Lee are good craftsmen but too innocent of the real world to do more than make a chronicle without emphasis or . . . No! There I go again, and I meant to make it up to Mr. Lawrence by saying that the story he told was not as distorted as I said it was. The cartoon was accurate.

5. NOTE TO "Strangers at Breakfast: *Five Finger Exercise*"

When I ran for office, a Poughkeepsie lady went rooting through the archives to get as many damaging quotations as she could from my work. It must have been a wearying task. Usually, the opposition stuck to the much-quoted "subversion of a society that bores and appalls me" to prove that I was — if not a Communist — at least in my own words "subversive." Curiously enough, this sort of thing does not do much damage. So much is said and whispered during a political campaign that only a few points ever get through to the electorate; in fact, sometimes one wonders if *anything* gets through. It is a chastening experience to find that after a year's steady campaigning in a district of 400,000 people, a large majority will go to the polls not knowing the name either of their Congressman or of his challenger. They will vote the party they have always voted.

In any case, this lady became one of my few really serious readers. Now it is usual, in current politics, to call people you are opposed to Communists. And with J. Edgar Hoover, the House Un-American Activities, the John Birch Society and the more sensational press honking their dread chorus, Communists do seem to be under every bed, in every other pulpit, devotedly infiltrating schools and legislatures. I don't know how

much the people in their general wisdom believe this
sort of thing. At the lower economic level they tend to
ignore name-calling. Sadly enough, it is the handsome
middle-aged ladies in hats and white gloves who will
tell you with deadly seriousness that they have absolute "proof" that Adlai Stevenson and Eleanor Roosevelt are card-carrying Communists.

My serious lady reader was not one of these. But she
was looking for heresy and she had an easy time of it.
She particularly enjoyed my gloomy remarks about the
family. For days she was on the telephone to friends,
reading the coda of the review of *Five Finger Exercise,*
adding: "And that's just the way the Communists feel
about the family." It is of course not at all the way the
Communists feel about the family. In Makarenkov's *A
Book for Parents,* the Soviet Spock rejoices: "Our family
is not an accidental combination of members of society.
The family is a natural collective body and, like everything natural, healthy and normal, it can only blossom
forth in Socialist society . . . . The family becomes the
natural primary cell of society, the place where the delight of human life is realized, where the triumphant
forces of man are refreshed, where children . . . the
chief joy of life . . . live and grow!" And on and on.
(Concurrently, the Soviet is much concerned over rising alcoholism, boredom and corruption. It would seem
that naturalness, health, normality and socialism are
not enough, even in that other Eden.)

Evidence does seem to indicate that since a third of

American marriages end in divorce, at least a third of our married population has no talent for marriage. Instead of denouncing those who find monogamy or togetherness or the raising of children difficult and unrewarding work, it might be more worthwhile to re-examine the whole moral, legal and economic basis of marriage and the family. Those who enjoy it and do it well should certainly be encouraged and admired. Those who have no gift for it should find other ways of fulfilling themselves. The idea that our parents or grandparents were "better" people because of the lower divorce rate in those days is nonsense. They were simply more effectively trapped than we. Divorce was socially unthinkable. There was not the ease of travel; there were few means whereby a woman could support herself and her children if she had to. But once women got political rights and were accepted as the work equals of men, the family as our ancestors knew it began to disintegrate. Now I would not be concerned with this dangerous (politically, that is) subject were it not for the children. Too many have been victimized by what passes for families, and they demonstrate every day in every tabloid what the absence of moral authority and of honesty in human relations (depicted so well in *Five Finger Exercise*) can do. Their response takes the form of juvenile delinquency, cynicism, contempt for others. They are, literally, de-moralized at having seen, close-to, a lie at work. Since most human beings are instinctively reactionary (it always seems simpler to try to go back to what one thought was a previous condition of society than to think ahead to something new), there is a bitter desire to punish those who fail to be good parents or make viable families. I think this is wrong. It is not human beings who are at fault in such matters but human institutions which have outlived their usefulness, at least for a large portion of the world. Ways should be found of raising the children of those who have not the interest — or talent — for raising children. To prepare for this, parental guilt should be exorcised; a guilty parent is worse than no parent. Eventually, a large percentage of the children will be brought up by the state. This sounds alarming. It is alarming. But the state need not be monstrous. At this very moment, thousands of families are far worse for the children in them than any institution would be. Optimistically, let us assume the task will be done well. What then? George Santayana, pondering such a future, struck off a phrase which haunts and chills me: the wolf pack. He saw the children brought up together, their allegiances not necessarily each to himself but to the pack he belonged to. Santayana found this vision of collective living as dreadful as I do; yet he did wonder at what new loyalties and new creativities might be released should the wolf pack succeed the solitary "I" of the postrenaissance West.

Meanwhile, our own society continues to denounce half its population for not making the tribal unit of prehistory work in a modern world where the patriarchal tribe is an anachronism. Somewhere between the ancient tribe and the unthinkable wolf pack there must be a proper way. If planning were not so counter to our national genius, I would suggest that those who know about these things begin the debate. But of course nothing will be done. In our refusal to plan anything, we are already constructing for ourselves not a free society but a cage.

What happened to the Poughkeepsie lady? Well, she is still keeping her scrapbooks. She will appreciate these remarks. "That's right, he said the children will be torn from the arms of their parents and put in concentration camps!" But there is some justice beneath the moon. I carried Republican Poughkeepsie by 1400 votes.

6.   NOTE TO "A Note on the Novel"

This piece caused some stir. It was misread, of course. I am still quoted as having said that the novel was dead. But I said no such thing. I merely pointed out that the large audience for the novel has gone away, and that is a fact. But as an art form the novel goes right on and in many ways it is healthier than ever.

Nevertheless, all the young men who are writing novels — most of the population, from what I can tell — challenged me. How could the novel be dead and the audience gone when young men are still writing novels with such hope and ferocity? My only answer is that the large audience is fickle, and that it was never written in stars that they would be enchanted forever by prose fictions of more than seventy thousand words. They prefer television, movies, the theater, adultery, alcohol, driving cars, any number of things to reading novels, and there is nothing to be done about it. Forget them. It is still enormously worthwhile to make something good, and there will always be those happy few who appreciate prose. All that has been lost (and this is what secretly hurts the ambitious young) is the nineteenth-century idea of the novelist as Folk Figure, enjoying world fame and attention. Hemingway was the last of these Folk Figures and I doubt if we shall see another one emerge from the ranks of the novelists. In fact, since Hemingway, those writers who have caught the world's attention have been novelists *manqué*, like Camus and Sartre. Each seized the center of the stage with autobiography, journalism, criticism, philosophy, theater. Each let the novel go before he had half explored it. Why? Because the urgent vision wants to affect. Novels, except as aids to masturbation, play no part in contemporary life. Their effect is small. The Folk Figures, the makers, the correctionists have turned to other ways. But this should not in any way depress the true novelist. All that he has lost is a kind of worldly fame and attention which, from Mark Twain to Ernest Hemingway, has usually done more harm to the man and the work than relative neglect ever did.

7. NOTE TO "Norman Mailer: The Angels Are White"

Since I wrote about Norman Mailer the reader of the *New York Daily News* has come to know his name altogether too well. It was said at the time of his arrest for assault I had seriously understated the matter when I wrote that he had "a nice but small gift for self-destruction." Of course one is almost always wrong in anticipating the course of any life, including one's own, and I have no urge to play prophet, especially in the case of Mailer. Yet I do think he will survive; at least I think he *ought* to survive; because for all his faults this society needs him.

Not unnaturally, he was piqued by what I wrote about him, though he took very well my complaints about his messianism and demagoguery. He did insist with masochistic pride that I was wrong when I claimed that he had made no *new* enemies in *Advertisements for Myself*. He felt he had made quite a few, particularly Saul Bellow. Therefore, I amend my statement accordingly.

Also, one should now draw attention to the fact that the age of General Eisenhower has drawn to a close. He is now one with General Grant, and not only is it possible to imagine an American President reading books, but we have now a President who reads everything, while many of the country's leaders are drawn from among its better minds. Things are looking up.

8. NOTE TO "Footnote to the Dreyfus Case"

I have always been fascinated by the Dreyfus case. At the time I wrote this review of Paléologue's journal, I was working on a film about Dreyfus for Metro-Goldwyn-Mayer. I put a good deal of effort into the script, especially into the moral debate. The result was a very bad movie called *I Accuse.* A number of talented people contributed to this disaster, as so often happens in a collective art form. I will not analyze the mistakes of others, only my own. I chose to tell the story from Dreyfus's point of view. Unfortunately, no matter how great one's sympathy for his dilemma, he was perhaps the least inspiring man ever to be involved in a great affair. As the center of an intricate morality play, he was worse than inadequate; he was ludicrous. But there is still a drama to be made out of the case, and I give one piece of advice to whatever successors I may have in that endeavor: tell the story from someone else's point of view. Keep Dreyfus in the background.

The essential foolishness of the man Dreyfus is beautifully revealed by a true story. The son of one of his friends was expelled from school for cheating. The friend was furious. He was certain that his son had not cheated. He appealed to Dreyfus. What did he think? After much thought, the man whose name is forever associated with the idea of justice said: "Well, where there's smoke, there's fire." As one of his defenders once remarked sourly, "Dreyfus is not a Dreyfusard."

9. NOTE TO "Writing Plays for Television"

I was wrong about everything. Personally, despite my boast that I was writing prose again, I soon found that I had become, inadvertently, a dramatist. In the years since this piece was written, I have been concerned with the theater and politics. The only prose I write is critical and journalistic — good exercise for the mind and for the spirit but not doing precisely what one ought to be doing. Although I don't agree with A. J. Liebling that most of the serous writers in our time turn finally to journalism, it is an obligatory form for those of us who would like to postpone the apocalypse.

As for television, despite the ritual reference to its fine abundance and the coming of a Golden Age of drama, I was far off the mark. By the end of the 1950's, original drama had largely vanished from the air. Nor does it show any immediate sign of reviving. The advertisers make more money with junk; and since the right to exploit others in the interest of making money is the only right the average American would lay down his life for, there will be little change in television. Yet I have always thought that one way of limiting the advertiser's control would be to establish in television the "magazine system." The advertiser would pay for his advertisement on the air, and that would be that. He would have no more control over programming than he has now over the editing of a magazine in which he buys space. The only other hope is paid television.

In 1961 I testified at the FCC hearings in New York and made certain points worth repeating here in brief. I said that I thought that the whole matter of advertising is one of the major moral issues in American society. The first thing most children are aware of is television. Knowing this, advertisers deliberately pervert nursery jingles to sell their products; the child learns the jingle, he sings it, he becomes a pitchman. To me that is exploitation of the most cynical kind.

Even worse is the national tolerance of falsehood. Sooner or later the child asks if the magic promised by the salesmen on television is true. Will he get big muscles if he eats a certain cereal? Of course not, his parents tell him. Those are just commercials. They are not true. In fact, the word "commercial" is now synonymous with misrepresentation. Therefore, the first thing the child notices in his society (and one of the most attractive) is false. He discovers that adults countenance deliberate falsehood. It is big business. If cynicism and contempt for the values of his society do not begin with this knowledge, the child is remarkable. More often, once he realizes that a great industry is based on falsity, he will take it for granted that everyone and everything — at least on television — is just as false, and when the President of the United States succeeds a commercial misrepresenting soap, he will take it for granted that the President is lying, too, in the interest of selling some political soap.

Finally, the advertiser is responsible for "the teen-ager." That phenomenon never existed until the advertisers, aware of the growing affluence of the adolescent, invented him. It was usual, in the previous America, to pass from childhood to adulthood with no more than a time of intervening awkwardness. Until the rise of American advertising, it never occurred to anyone anywhere in the world that the teen-ager was a captive in a hostile world of adults, with his own morality and language, his difference from the world of adults a source of pride.

One of the few extant private statements of Shakespeare is relevant. The boy actors of London were in commercial and artistic competition with the adult popular theater. Because the boy actors had the more powerful patrons (and the greater prestige), they were able to make a good deal of professional mischief for grownup actors. When asked what he thought of this competitiveness, Shakespeare observed mildly that boy actors must remember that one day they will be men actors, and suffer in maturity for the deeds of their youth. The American teen-ager, as the advertiser has created him, is encouraged to think of himself as a being apart, sensitive and misunderstood, a rebel with a definite cause: to get even with the adult world in one way or another (preferably by overconsumption) while delaying as long as possible the dreaded passage to maturity. At every turn the adolescent as consumer is flattered and reminded of his precious estate. To cause division between age groups is something new under the sun. American advertising has achieved it.

10. NOTE TO "A Note on *The Best Man*"

The success of *The Best Man* was a surprise to me. I was not at all confident that audiences would accept the bleakness of the political observation. In the play's first version, I allowed the opportunist Senator Cantwell to win. The good man was too weak, the bad man too tough. The play was black and I was quite willing to fight the battle to keep it so (and enjoy almost certain popular failure) if I had been entirely convinced that a man as bad as Senator Cantwell could get elected. After much thought I changed my mind. Cantwell could not prevail — at least nowadays — because in its idiot way our system, though it usually keeps us from having the very best man as President, does protect us from the very worst. That is two cheers for democracy, as E. M. Forster would say, and I was willing to make them.

Even more than courage, intelligence, and charisma, the Presidency requires of its occupant the proper temperament. I have always thought of *The Best Man* as a study in temperament. Three politicians, each in his way gifted, are revealed. Yet only one (the former President) is possessed of the proper temperament for the great task, that curious knowledge of when to modify opportunism with principle, the intuitive sense, finally, of moral priority.

Contrary to rumor, I was not writing about Adlai Stevenson, Richard Nixon and Harry Truman. There were elements of these men in each of the characters, but no more. At a crucial moment in our history I wanted to present to an audience of voters a small essay in Presidential temperament. It is interesting that the politicians themselves should have been so taken with the play. Mr. Truman summed it up backstage at the Morosco Theater one night when he said to the actor who had been playing the part of a former President not unlike himself: "I've known so many politicians like you!"